The Land and People of
KENYA

PORTRAITS OF THE NATIONS SERIES

ALSO IN THE SAME FORMAT

The Land and People of
KENYA

Edna Mason Kaula

PORTRAITS OF THE NATIONS SERIES

J. B. LIPPINCOTT COMPANY
Philadelphia and New York

Map by the author

*Grateful acknowledgment is made to the Kenya Mission to the United
Nations for assistance in the preparation of this book.*

*The author wishes to thank the following for permission to use the photographs
in this book:*

The African-American Institute: page 98.

B.O.A.C.: page 75.

Columbia Pictures Corporation: page 129.

David Davies: page 114.

Department of Information, Nairobi, Kenya: page 54.

East Africa Tourist Travel Association: page 47.

Ronald D. K. Hadden: pages 117, 119 (top and bottom).

George Holton, U.N.I.C.E.F.: page 53.

Kenya Information Services: pages 13, 15, 16, 17 (top), 19, 20, 21, 26, 27, 29,
37, 39, 40, 42, 45, 63, 73, 79, 85, 87, 88, 89, 90, 105, 110, 116.

Kenya Public Relations Department: page 30.

Kenya Tourist Office: pages 17 (bottom), 24, 28, 76, 123, 124.

Alastair Matheson, U.N.I.C.E.F.: pages 106, 107.

New York Zoological Society: page 127.

United Nations: pages 49, 66, 78, 83, 41, 96, 100.

For Alouise Boker
Because she likes Kenya

CONTENTS

The Land and People of
KENYA

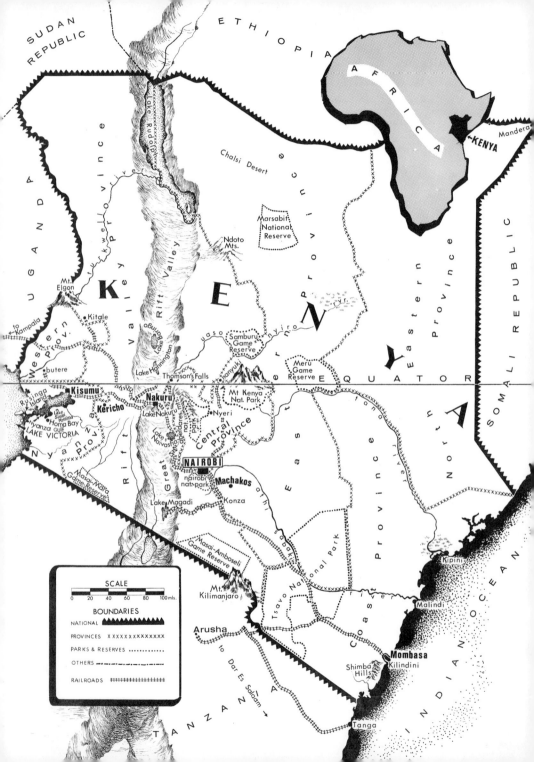

1

HIGH HILLS
AND DEEP VALLEYS

"He who has tasted honey will return to the honey pot" is an East African saying that is applicable to the Republic of Kenya, an exceptionally beautiful land, full of excitement and variety. Only a rare, unimaginative visitor is unaffected by Kenya's enchantment; nearly everyone yearns to return; and a few remain to become Kenyan citizens.

The Republic of Kenya has been an independent nation since December 12, 1963. It is located on the eastern seaboard of Africa and covers 225,000 square miles of territory, which is almost equal in size to Texas. Kenya borders the Sudan Republic and Ethopia to the north, the Somalia Republic and the Indian Ocean to the east, Tanzania to the south, and Lake Victoria and Uganda to the west.

Though Kenya straddles the equator and two-thirds of the land is uncultivable, the climate is temperate because of an adequate rainfall and high mountains. Most parts of Kenya enjoy two rainfalls—the "long rains" from March to May, and the "short rains" during November and December. Only the desert regions to the north and northeast are consistently hot for they have hardly any rainfall at all.

Majestic mountain ranges rise in southern and central Kenya. The temperature on these highlands varies from a mean maximum of 82 degrees Fahrenheit (February) to a mean minimum of about 53 degrees (June and July). Trade winds that blow in off the Indian Ocean relieve the humidity of the low-lying coastal area where the mean maximum temperature is 90 degrees and the mean minimum temperature is 68.5 degrees.

A good way to understand Kenya and to appreciate its variety is to go on an imaginary journey through the country's seven provinces.

The *Coast Province* faces the Indian Ocean across 380 miles of shorefront. Miles of gently sloping beaches, whitened with fine sand, are broken by placid lagoons sheltered between coral reefs. The main concentration of East Africa's reefs is off the Kenya-Tanzania coast. Coral is a primitive marine animal that grows beneath the surface of the water. As new coral grows, it pushes the old, lifeless coral to the surface. At low tide only, the varied, subtle pastel hues of this dead coral is visible. Very much alive are vividly colored, oddly shaped starfish and crustaceans that lie on the sandy floors of deep coral pools off Kenya's coast. Lining the shorefront are forests of palm trees that bend before a brisk ocean breeze.

Kenya's longest river, the Tana, flows into the Indian

Coconuts are trade items along East Africa's coast.

Ocean, as does the Sabaki River which is called the Athi River where it rises in the central mountains. Both rivers suffer from annual flooding when the people who live by them are marooned for several weeks. And because of their shallowness, neither river is navigable except for small craft.

Other rivers in Kenya are the Uaso Nyiro which flows from the highlands northeast to peter out in hot, papyrus-fringed swamplands, the Turkwell River which flows north into Lake Rudolph, and several small rivers which empty into Lake Victoria.

To penetrate Kenya's *Rift Valley Province* you leave the coconut palms and cultivated fields of sugar and sisal and journey west, parallel to the Sabaki River, into a stretch of flat country. Here only thornbush and flat-topped acacias survive. Rocks and anthills throw long shadows. There are no tall trees, for the gradually rising, rolling, and ravine-creased plain is sterile and parched for the need of water. Patches of red, gritty soil gape from between wiry grass clumps like fresh wounds.

But after crossing Tsavo National Park—which almost equals Massachusetts in size and, next to the Ethosha Game Reserve in Southwest Africa, is the largest national park in the world—you enter dense jungle country in the Rift Valley Province and are rewarded with one of Kenya's grandest views. Although Mount Kilimanjaro (19,340 feet high and Africa's tallest mountain) rises in Tanzania immediately south of Kenya's border, its breathtaking grandeur stands perpetually for Kenyans to enjoy. The mountain's peak looms across the plains. At times clouds cover it and little wisps of violet light hover about its snow-covered glaciers. In Kenyan territory the trees of the forest below the snowline grow so closely together and are so thickly foliaged that it seems as though one could walk on their tops. The forests are cut by the valleys of watercourses that come down into lush vegetation out of the thick timber on the mountain.

The view of Kilimanjaro is merely a foretaste of the beauties that the Rift Valley Province has to offer. They include green farmlands, bamboo forests, and mountain moorlands that reach up to 14,000 feet in height and extend from Kenya's southern to its northern borders where Lake Rudolph touches Ethiopia. Rudolph is Kenya's largest lake.

Mt. Kilimanjaro looms above the Kenyan plains.

Except for a short stretch of shoreline that touches Ethiopia it is wholly within Kenya. The lake stretches for 180 miles, north to south, and covers an area of 2,473 square miles.

The Rift Valley is a geological phenomenon that is repeated nowhere else on earth. It is a mighty chasm that begins in the foothills of Turkey's mountains and runs through Jordan and East Africa as far south as Malawi. Unlike the usual conception of a valley, in most places the Rift is a hot dry plain. Underfoot it is either volcanic rubble or red powdery stretches that are the remains of lakes of former wetter periods. In Kenya the Rift Valley is more fertile, and in parts is twenty to forty miles wide and two to three thousand feet below the surface of the surrounding country. In some places sheer precipices rise from either side of the Rift.

Shallow lakes string through the Rift like iridescent gems

Overlooking the Great Rift Valley.

shining against a hazy purple background. Towards Kenya's south the lake waters are alkaline—which attracts a species of pink flamingoes. Along the shore of one lake, Nakuru, flamingoes form a band 50 yards wide that extends for two or three miles. Lake Magadi, near the Tanzania border, is the world's largest source of soda ash and salt. The lake yields about $3 million worth of soda a year, most of which is exported to South Africa.

The thickly wooded Aberdare Mountain Range rises to the east of the Rift. It extends for about 100 miles and reaches heights of 13,000 feet. From the western rim of the Rift, the land slopes down towards Lake Victoria and Uganda where Mount Elgon rises to 14,178 feet. Here are rich farmlands that grow wheat, corn, and dairy products.

The Rift Valley Province shares Mount Elgon with Uganda and the *Western Province*. The Western Province

Flamingoes along the shore of Lake Nakuru.

The flat-topped summit of Mt. Elgon, seen from the edge of the forest.

also shares Lake Victoria (the world's second largest fresh-water lake) with Uganda, Tanzania, and with *Nyanza Province*.

Although Lake Victoria is approximately 3,720 feet above sea level and the nights are cooled by lake breezes, the sunlight hours in this area are hot. The lakeshore is deeply indented with narrow, twisted bays where fishing boats drag their nets while trailed by thousands of colorful waterfowl. Small ferries carry goods and passengers to offshore islands. On one island, Rusinga, the remains of one of man's earliest ancestors from the Miocene age was discovered many years ago.

In 1931, Dr. L. S. B. Leakey, the Kenya-born Director of the Corydon Museum in Nairobi, landed on Rusinga Island and immediately found a fossil jawbone of a Miocene terrestrial ape. It was the first of several hundreds that have since been found in the vicinity of Lake Victoria. Twenty million years ago the lake's contour was different from what it is today. The water extended farther into Kenya, and man's ancestors came to drink along its shores. But gradually the ash from neighboring active volcanoes filled the lake. The ash, combined with clay and sandstone in which the fossils are found, contained an unknown ingredient that acted as a fossilizing preservative which has made the task of identification easier for diggers.

Quite close to Lake Victoria is a crater lake, Simbi Nyaima, at one time the site of a thriving village. But, according to Nyanza legends, it was submerged by heavy rains and sank. *Simbi* means "sunken village," and *Nyaima* means "disaster."

Directly to the south of the Western Province is *Nyanza Province*, a colorful patchwork of small holdings that cover rolling slopes containing tea plantations, and on higher ground of what appear as white daisies. This is pyrethrum which, when plucked and dried and exported to Europe, makes a base for insecticides such as DDT.

On this imaginary inspection of Kenya's provinces, you will fly over the Rift Valley to the *North Eastern Province*. What a contrast to the rolling green hills and lush valleys, the high-rising mountains and cascading waterfalls of previously visited areas! The North Eastern Province shares a 450-mile-long borderline with Somalia. Most of the province is flat, monotonous, rock-strewn desert. It is land that nature has filed down to bare rock. Yet pastoralists leading camels

Studying the pyrethrum crop at Egerton College, Njoro.

herd their lean cattle among spiky thornbush and brittle yellow grasses that a hot wind blows in waves on infrequent hillsides. The soil is poor and sterile—quite unsuitable for cultivation, though towards the south are plantations of gray-green sisal whose tops are as sharp as needles.

The bleak, windswept moorlands continue into the *Eastern Province*, though mountain ranges and solitary peaks rise near Lake Rudolph to relieve the monotonous landscape. But as you move towards the gradually rising southern area you come to magnificent forest and mountain scenery. Mount Kenya rises in the middle of the jungle. It is Kenya's highest mountain (the second highest in Africa), reaching to 17,058 feet. Its jagged twin peaks, Batian and Nelion, glisten in an endless, changing play of light that forms and

Camels graze near Lake Rudolph.

reforms cloud and shadow and transmutes the black-rock faces and tooth-edged crags into something as airy and ethereal as butterflies. In the midnight blue of night, light from stars as close-packed as pebbles on a beach gleam on the snowcapped peaks. Johannes Rebmann and Johann Ludwig Krapf, two German missionaries and the first known Europeans to have seen Mount Kenya, met ridicule and disbelief when they reported having seen "snow on the equator." The first party to conquer the mountain was led by Sir Halford MacKinder, who reached the top on September 13, 1899.

Mount Kenya borders the *Central Province*, the core of Kenya, the heart of the highlands to which visitors gravitate and from which safaris set out on exciting expeditions

Mt. Kenya, the highest peak in Kenya and the second highest in Africa.

to view Kenya's bountiful supply of wild game. The Central Province averages about 5,000 feet above sea level. The sky is crystal clear, the sunshine hard and bright. The fragrance of flowering trees and African freezias perfume the air.

The late Danish writer, Isak Dinesen, has perhaps preserved in her writings the truest picture of Kenya. She lived on a 6,000-acre farm 6,000 feet up in the highlands for almost seventeen years. When the coffee market slumped in 1931, she sold her farm and went back to Denmark to relive her Kenya years by writing of them. When Isak Dinesen vividly describes a landscape like "the colors in pottery," or the flowers that grow in the "wilderness of game country," in imagination one can see and smell them. Isak Dinesen's books about Kenya and its people will always be acclaimed as masterful interpretations of an idyllic way of life in an unspoiled land.

Though cities and towns dot Kenya's land at strategic points, either for commerce or shipping or merely for sightseeing, it comes as no surprise that Kenyans chose to build their capital city, Nairobi, in the beautiful setting that is the Central Province.

2

OLD CITIES
AND NEW TOWNS

Nature gave Kenya its magnificent mountains, its lakes, and its abundance of forests and wildlife, but men created the cities and towns. Kenya's modern cities are symbols of independent Africa; they stand as monuments to the second half of the twentieth century and freedom from colonialism; they represent the hopes of a fast-developing new nation that is taking its place in today's world.

Long before Nairobi was the capital of Kenya, pastoralists who grazed their cattle on the site called it *Nakuso-Ntelon*—"The beginning of all beauty." They named the stream where they watered their cattle *Nairobi*—"The cool water."

Nairobi the capital started life in 1900 as a siding when the British were building a railroad from the coast to Kampala in Uganda. It was the last spot where locomotives could

An aerial view of Nairobi, capital of Kenya.

shunt before reaching the mountainous highlands. (The snows from Mount Kenya—seventy miles distant—are still tapped and piped to steam locomotives that chug up the steep inclines from Mombasa.)

From a sleepy, struggling town, Nairobi has grown into a bustling, modern city, the safari capital of the world and the commercial hub of East Africa. Kenyans are razing some buildings of European design because they are unhappy reminders of when Kenya was a British colony. Today's Nairobi could be a modern city anywhere in America or Europe, for it gleams with many chrome and glass-fronted buildings. Tree-lined streets relieve the stark effect. Eucalypti spread their fragrance, and when jacaranda blossoms fall they provide a purple carpet for pedestrians. A new Government House faces a spacious park, dotted with bougainvillea and hibiscus shrubs in varying hues, and the Parliament Buildings have recently been extended in a wide sweep under a tall clock-tower. With such signs of growth, the city responds with vitality to the promise of a new, prosperous era.

Nairobi's population count reached 350,000 when the city's boundaries were recently expanded to include new housing projects. Of this number the vast majority are of course Africans, though about 90,000 Indian merchants and 20,000 Europeans share the delights of modern theaters, art galleries, museums, libraries, nightclubs, cafes, and twenty churches, synagogues, and mosques.

In addition, every year about 150,000 visitors find pleasure in meeting the variety of the region's friendly people, the superb scenery, the balmy climate, and, foremost, the wild animals that live right at Nairobi's "back door." United States citizens are numbered among the visitors. A post set up at the airport with signs pointing to thirty-five leading world cities reminds them that they are a long way from home. From Nairobi to New York measures 7,356 miles.

Mombasa, on a small island set in a sheltering bay off the coast where the railroad starts, is Kenya's second largest city and the country's chief seaport. *Mombasa* means "The Island of War"—a fitting name—for Mombasa was the scene of conflicts between Africans and Arabs as long ago as the sixth century, and between the Arabs and the Portuguese during the sixteenth and seventeenth centuries. One massive structure, Fort Jesus, still stands in Mombasa. Built by Portuguese conquerors, its pink walls are grim reminders of

The Kilindini Road in Mombasa, the chief seaport.

East Africa's darkest period. Today, Fort Jesus serves as a museum.

Mombasa is more Arab in aspect than African. If you took a walk through one of the narrow, winding streets in the Old Town, you would see overhanging, ornately carved balconies that are typically Arabic, and solid oaken doorways that have acquired a silken patina through centuries of use. Stand under a vivid blue sky on the shore of Mombasa's Old Harbor and you will see high-pooped lateen-sailed Arab dhows, designed for long sea voyages and manned by turbaned, bearded Arabs, either sailing in if the northeast monsoon winds are blowing (November), or setting off for Arabia, Persia, Greece, and India, if the trade winds blow from the southwest (March and April). These mer-

A race between high-pooped, lateen-rigged Arab dhows.

chant sailors bring figs and dates, dried fish and salt, building tiles, carpets, and ornaments. They take away mangrove poles from nearby swamplands, cottons, and light machinery.

There is also a modern Mombasa with a harbor, Kilindini, that caters to modern, mechanized shipping, an airport, and a seaplane landing.

A 1962 census gave Mombasa's population totaling about 112,000 Africans, 44,000 Asians, 18,000 Arabs, 5,000 Europeans, and 1,000 others.

One branch of the railroad terminates at Kisumu on the Nyanza Gulf, Lake Victoria. Kisumu is Kenya's "granary," as it is the marketing center for a wide variety of cash crops. Corn, cotton, coffee, sisal, sugarcane, bananas, and peanuts are exported from Kisumu. The busy markets throb with

The old harbor in Mombasa.

sound, for Kisumu is also the distributing point for the fishing fleets—long, slim sailing craft that bring their catch into the markets—and for big diesel-engined cruisers that voyage around the lake. Of more than 22,000 inhabitants, Indians predominate. They can be seen applying their talents as traders before open stalls in the Kisumu markets.

Kenya has "planned" towns that are spectacular in their growth. Homa Bay, across the Nyanza Gulf from Kisumu was, in 1962, a picturesque small village. It is now the headquarters for the South Nyanza District, serving 482,000 people with a modern hospital, a modern high school, a modern postal system, and handsome new churches and missions. In 1967, the town's supply of electricity was extended to aid in operating a new, large, farmers' training center, which was built and equipped by funds given by the people of Sheffield, England, through a Freedom from Hunger campaign.

A visitor to Homa Bay is still greeted by mingled sounds of singing workmen, hammering carpenters, and unloading truckmen. The town planners are preparing accommodations for guests who come to Kisumu in increasing numbers to enjoy the sports of fishing and sailing that the lake offers, a new bird sanctuary close by, and other attractions contained within the province.

Moving east from Homa Bay one passes *Kericho*—meaning "The place of the medicine man"—where an aroma of drying tea leaves hangs heavily in the air. This pretty town, surrounded by fertile lands, is the center of Kenya's tea

Homa Bay on Lake Victoria.

industry. Fifty miles further east is the west rim of the Rift Valley. Descending into the Rift you find Lake Nakuru with its vast bird population, creating a shimmering pink atmosphere that is repeated in the feather-speckled water.

Right there, bordering the lake and beside the railroad, sits Nakuru the town. Although it lies in the heart of the Rift, Nakuru is 6,071 feet above sea level. It is the trading center of the highlands. On Saturdays, Nakuru's population, which is some 38,000 of several races, is swelled by farmers who bring in their produce to sell, and other outsiders who come to replenish their stocks of foodstuffs.

Nakuru is an active, thriving township. It has many new buildings that include a modern railroad station painted in

A tea estate in the Highlands.

red and black, a blanket factory, a flour mill, and an impressive bank building.

Due east from Nakuru, up the Rift escarpment and over the Aberdare Mountains, Nyeri is situated within sight of Mount Kenya. Though small, the town is growing fast and is of great importance to Kenya. Nyeri is the Provincial headquarters of the Central Province, the administrative center for a large farming project, and the point to which visitors gravitate. The Treetops Hotel, adjacent to Nyeri, enjoys world fame as the converging point for visitors also, of whom 95 percent are foreign tourists. From treetops balconies they thrill with delight at the sight of elephant herds and other big game busy at natural salt licks. In 1952, England's Queen Elizabeth II (then the Duchess of Edinburgh) shared the pleasures of Treetops with the Duke the night before she learned of the death of her father, King George VI.

Despite Nyeri's present rapid growth, the small town retains a serene atmosphere in its beautiful mountain setting. In the heart of the town stands a memorial to the men who fought for freedom during the period from 1951 to 1957. Close by is another memorial—the grave of Lord Baden-Powell who was the founder of the Boy Scout Movement. Groups of scouts from distant countries come to Nyeri to pay respect to their late leader.

Towns have mushroomed all over Kenya, but the story of the development of Machakos from a stretch of land that resembled desert after successive years of drought and over-cultivation to a modern, booming town and district has been described as the "greatest miracle in Africa."

Machakos lies forty miles to Nairobi's south. Less than eighty years ago the British East Africa Company erected a fort in the town as a prime strategic point where its administrators "established law and order in Ukambani"—the name for a previous Kenya province. In 1922, the fort was demolished. Today, only one gate post remains to mark the spot. But Machakos clings to local African history. Many years ago a famous witch doctor, Masaku, lived on the site of the present administrative offices. Machakos authority calls itself the Masaku County Council in order to perpetuate his name.

Not only is Machakos's civil service almost completely Africanized, but education, trade, and industry are also. Some credit goes to students of the Kenya Israel College of Social Workers which, in 1962, the Israeli Government gave to the district. Students seek out homeless children throughout the countryside and bring them to a residential youth center. They apply the spark of pride to rural families to work harder in the fields; they cultivate an interest in unity, in combined efforts to improve the villages in order to raise their living standards.

With an area of 6,000 square miles, rich soil, an average rainfall of about thirty-five inches, and a population of 570,000 ambitious people, Machakos sheds the scourge of poverty. Like other new Kenyan cities and towns, Machakos looks to a future of greater and greater production through its own human efforts.

Such are samples of Kenya's cities and towns. There are many more. Throughout the mountains and across the deserts little towns and villages dot the landscape like succulent fruit on a wild fig tree.

But what of Kenya's people to whom cities and towns are the honey pots, and who are responsible for their phenomenal growth? It is also important to know who the people are, where they came from, what history lies behind them.

3

KENYA'S PEOPLE

Thousands of African families have forsaken their rural lives to share the excitement that cities offer. By doing so they have created social problems and complicated food production. But the great bulk of Kenya's people still live in country districts.

Almost 10 million people inhabit Kenya. Of this number about 188,000 are Asian, 36,000 are Arab, and 49,000 are European. The majority of Kenyans are Africans who are divided into four main groups—Bantu, Nilotic, Nilo-Hamitic, and Hamitic, which together comprise about forty-six separate tribes. Each tribe speaks its own dialect, but the Government of the new Republic of Kenya wisely stresses the importance of creating an awareness of national unity. It encourages the people to speak a common language, Swahili, which evolved from a mixture of Arabic (when Arabs controlled the coast), a little Portuguese, Galla (from the Horn of Africa), and several local languages.

The four main African tribal groups were not always in Kenya. The true indigenes are few in number. One tribe, the Dorobo, is reduced to about one hundred families. They are sturdy people, clad in animal skins, and are almost as small as the pygmies. Dorobo men, who hunt with bow and poisoned arrow, have a remarkable knowledge of the flora and fauna they find in the dense cedar mountain forests where they live. Legend credits the Dorobo with being every man's ancestor. In the beginning, according to the legend, a Dorobo gave birth to a boy and a girl who issued from his shinbone. And thus the human race began.

The origin of the El Molo tribe (whose name means Poor Devils) is also unknown. Anthropologists believe that they are survivals of a primitive race that peopled East Africa long before the arrival of today's Kenyans. Fewer than one hundred men, women, and children live in crude dwellings among the lava rocks on the barren shores of Lake Rudolph. They wear little clothing in the furnacelike heat. Their tools are long fish spears for they are expert fishermen. The El Molos' monotonous diet consists of the fish with which the lake is richly stocked, but the high alkaline content of Lake Rudolph is responsible for ailments that afflict them and that are gradually reducing El Molo numbers. Yet nothing will persuade them to abandon their homes for more comfortable surroundings in the south.

The members of another indigenous tribe, El Kony, herd goats on Mount Elgon, 11,000 feet above sea level, which is higher than the forest line. At one time the El Kony lived in caves lower on the mountain where the woods are thick, but invading tribes pushed them skyward. Still another true indigenous group is the sparsely scattered Waliangula people who inhabit the arid scrubland towards Kenya's coast. The men are crackerjack marksmen with bow and arrow, using strong, mysterious poisons for killing elephants and other big game.

The history of Kenya's first inhabitants is unknown; so, too, is much of the history of Kenya's people today. Although Arabs were active traders along East Africa's coast since the beginning of the Christian era, no detailed record remains of Kenya's interior activities. But it is known that a series of mass movements of tribal groups surged into Kenya between the twelfth and seventeenth centuries. There were three major migrations, one from West and Central Africa, from which stem the Bantu tribes, a second from the vicinity of the Sudan, North Africa, which brought the Nilotes, and a third from Northeast Africa, possibly Southern Arabia, which introduced the Hamites.

The name of the fourth tribal group, Nilo-Hamitic, is really a misnomer for it implies a mixture of Nilotic and Hamitic. But the Nilo-Hamitic language bears no similarity to those of the Nilotes and Hamites. The name Nilo-Hamitic was adopted to describe the nine tribes of nomadic herdsmen of which the Masai are the best known. They entered Kenya from the vicinity of Lake Rudolph during the eighteenth and nineteenth centuries.

No doubt fierce battles, conquests, defeats, and annihilations resulted from the meeting and clashing of differing groups until the tribes settled into the distribution as we know it today.

The Bantu people far outnumber Kenya's other ethnic

Masai warriors, armed with only a spear and shield, hunt lions.

groups, accounting for 65 percent of the people. Character-
istic of most of the Bantu is that they prefer to farm on the
mountain slopes. The Kikuyu, whose people farm around
the base of Mount Kenya, is the largest Bantu tribe in
Kenya. They worship the mountain and preserve their origin
in a romantic legend.

When their original leader, Kikuyu, led his people into
Kenya from the west, he stopped when he came to the
highlands. Then Ngai, the Divider of the Universe, appeared
and beckoned Kikuyu to follow him to his home on the

mountaintop. From there Ngai designated the boundaries within which Kikuyu and his people could live. He pointed to a grove of wild fig trees and ordered Kikuyu to build his home right there. Ngai also advised Kikuyu to sacrifice an animal and call to the mountain should he ever need help. Kikuyu descended the mountain and found a beautiful wife waiting for him when he reached the grove of fig trees. Her name was Moombi. During the tranquil years that followed, Moombi had nine daughters. Kikuyu loved his little girls but he longed for a son. He feared he would have no descendants to sing praise-poems to his memory, for it is a son's duty and privilege to appeal to ancestor spirits with praise-poems which he has composed. So Kikuyu sacrificed an animal and called his needs to the mountaintop. Ngai saw the sacrifice and heard the appeal. He sent nine young men for Kikuyu's daughters, the tribe was established, and Kikuyu's place in the spirit world was assured.

Each of the nine foremost Bantu tribes differ slightly in appearance and dress, but the Wakamba people are of particular interest because only recently they made a dramatic change in their centuries-old customs. Previously they were fighters, now they are farmers. They have laid aside the long bow and taken up the hoe and plow. Once, a Wakamba young man's ambition was to enlist in Kenya's army, prison, or police force; now he strives to learn and to adopt modern farming methods. The Wakamba are the people who live in the Machakos district. It was under the guidance of Kenya's former government, the British, that they were prompted into transforming the deserts of Machakos into thriving, productive farmlands. When the Wakamba take time off

Acrobatic Wakamba dancers.

from developing their land, they express their happiness in wild, imaginative dancing, for they are a cheerful, independent people.

Of about seven different Nilotic tribes in Kenya, the Luo is the largest. Their people number more than one million, making them second to the Kikuyu in size. *Luo* means "People of the swamp," for they came from the swamp country of the Upper Nile River. One anthropologist compared the Luo migration as being like a line of shunting freight cars, each car representing a tribe that shoved similar tribes backwards and forwards as they struggled to claim their rich fertile shores of Lake Victoria. Today the Luo people are well established in the lake region where they fish and farm. Theirs is one of the most densely populated areas in Africa.

The Nilo-Hamitic group occupies territory that extends from Lake Rudolph through the Rift Valley and its adjacent highlands, south into Tanzania. The proud Masai are the most southernly situated, having been until recently the most aggressive. Equally colorful are the Samburu of northern Kenya who call themselves "the world's top people." They cling to most of their time-tried customs, though they have seriously adopted the practice of modern animal husbandry. This has won fame for them as nomadic cattle herders, for today 50,000 Samburu own 350,000 humpbacked cattle which produce good beef. The Samburu are tough, strong people who can walk long distances with neither food nor water and, like the Masai and other Nilo-Hamitic tribesmen, they can kill lions with only their spears.

Of the four principal Hamitic tribes, the Somali are the most prominent—in numbers and sagacity. The word *So-*

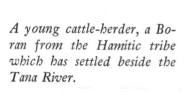

A young cattle-herder, a Boran from the Hamitic tribe which has settled beside the Tana River.

mali comes from two Arabic words—*zu* and *mal*—meaning "possessors of great wealth." The name is appropriate, for Somali wealth is measured by the size of their herds of cattle, camels, and goats, regardless of how ill-nourished these animals might be. Originally the Somali spilled into Kenya from Somalia in search of grazing grounds. The 280,000 Somali who are Kenyan nationals roam over the arid country in the northeast that is mainly composed of barren rock and thorny scrub, and to the south as far as the Tana River.

Kenya's four linguistic groups are drawing closer as they become proficient in speaking the Swahili language that originated through the intermingling of Kenya's Arab citizens with Africans. Arabs, clothed in their traditional long white *kanzus*, still choose to hug the coast. They are occupied mainly as fishermen and seamen, though there are a few who work in factories or on their own small farms.

Visitors to Kenya are surprised to see such large numbers of Asians, not only in the cities, but also in the most remote distant villages. They are descendants of workers whom the British brought to Kenya from India for constructing the first railroad. Life was easier in the new land than in crowded India and many workers remained in Kenya when their contracts expired. They made a living as shopkeepers—both retail and wholesale—and as moneylenders and money changers. They imported merchandise never before seen in Africa, such as sewing machines, blankets, and lamps—and matches to light them by. The Indians set up tiny shops called *dukas*. They were also tailors, and a sewing machine was an essential part of their equipment. Many Indians grew fabulously rich and were able to send money

An Indian visitor (left) helps inspect the maize or corn crop.

home regularly to their poor relations in India. Before Africans gained business experience they were sometimes the victims of unfair Indian practices so that the very presence of Indians created tensions.

After Kenya won independence the lot of the 200,000 or so Indians and Pakistani residents steadily worsened. When granting Independence in 1963, Britain had offered them a choice of becoming either British or Kenyan citizens. The majority of the Asians chose British citizenship. At first, only a few Indians left Kenya, but when the Kenya Government started on a strict Africanization program by withdrawing work permits for aliens, the flow of immigrants to Britain rapidly increased and had risen to 3,000 monthly by February, 1968. Britain's social services were strained beyond the limit and Mr. Harold Wilson, the Prime Minister, saw a need to act. He and his Cabinet produced an emergency bill that was driven through Parliament in three days. Starting on March 1, 1968, the bill allowed only 1,500 Kenya Indians, plus their dependents, to enter Britain annually. Prior to the deadline, Indians jammed the Nairobi airport in a frantic effort to leave Kenya. And harsh criticism was directed towards Britain's Labor Government. Mrs. Eirene White, vice-chairman of the Labor Party, said that the British Government had broken its word and devalued its passport— "but," she added, "the restrictions had been necessary."

The status of Europeans living in Kenya has reversed since independence. Where they once directed trade and politics they now have little or no authoritative voice. Though many Europeans still control much of Kenya's business and industry while others farm, almost as many have left the country. The majority of Kenya's European citizens came from Britain and to Britain they returned.

But like Kenya's diverse tribespeople who are learning to live together in harmony, so are the Asians and Europeans who are now Kenya citizens, and the Africans, for each has something to contribute to the future of the country that was once a British colony. Kenyans are trying to avoid the mistakes made by some new African states such as the Congo and Nigeria, where rivalry between the tribes has brought about tragic revolution.

All peoples in Kenya are learning, regardless of differing ethnic backgrounds, that they are members of one nation, the Republic of Kenya.

4

CHANGING CUSTOMS

Kenya's Government is as anxious to preserve customs and traditions that are beneficial to the people and that add to their welfare as it is to unite them with a common language. It is launched on an educational program that will do away with superstitious practices that are destructive, that terrorize their victims, and undermine confidence. Already, many Kenyans who have gone to live in towns and cities are detribalized and have abandoned old beliefs. But the lives of many thousands more are still untouched by an alien civilization. They live very much as their parents and grandparents did before them.

Kenyan customs are as diversified as the more than forty tribal groups that practice them, though each tribe follows traditions concerned with its common basic needs, which are grazing grounds and water.

Some customs of the Kipsigis tribe can serve as examples of a people who stand with one foot in the primitive past and the other in the progressive present. Also, more Kipsigis land was alienated by the early British settlers than that of other tribal people because it lay in a rich farmland region. The Kipsigis are of Nilo-Hamitic origin and consider themselves "brothers" to the Nandi Keyo, Suk, and Turen tribes with whom they share the Kalenjin language. Their traditional enemies were, until recently, the Masai (though of Nilo-Hamitic origin also), and the Nilotic Luo who are their neighbors.

The Kipsigis live on 997 square miles of undulating high land southeast of Kisumu, and they number 350,000. An adequate rainfall keeps their fields green, their clear streams burbling. The corn rises tall and strong, tea bushes grow thick and bushy, wild flowers bloom in the rich, red soil.

A Kipsigis elder from the Kericho district.

Traditionally the land was the property of the tribes; now it has become, as in other countries, the property of individuals. In contrast to the nomadic custom of following their cattle, the Kipsigis have seized the opportunity an ambitious government offered them and have become the first generation of landowners. Usually each family owns between twenty and fifty acres which they pay for in installments. And to conform to an old Kenya saying, "He who has land must have labor," half of them employ paid labor, which is nearly always drawn from the Luo.

A sense of family is embedded in the tall, thin-lipped, copper-colored Kipsigis people as strongly as trees in their earthen beds, and a fine network of relationships comprise a household which includes aunts, cousins, in-laws, and many children. This is true of every African group. Good manners are maintained between family members, particularly in the use of terms of address, for Kenyans move through life in age groups, each with its own formal salutation.

When the Kipsigis were cattle-herders only, the family answered to the will of the father, for he owned the cattle. He once had the leisure to sit with his peers, sipping beer from a common calabash through a flexible reed quite six feet long. The contented elders drank and chatted while their wives and daughters worked. The women trudged through the fields, their backs bent under huge loads of firewood suspended by straps of hide that pressed into their foreheads. Their clothing consisted of small leather aprons which drooped and made them appear as slow-moving brown beetles. Sons, when beyond the age to mind the cattle (which it was the women's duty to milk) were trained to

Somali women at the wells.

be warriors. They passed their days practicing spear-throwing when they were not occupied in grooming their bodies with butter and red clay, or braiding one another's hair into numerous tiny pigtails.

A father's authority is reduced to a fraction of what it was since a new system enables sons and daughters to cooperate in working the farm and thus benefit from proceeds that bring them independence. The head of a family now takes his place alongside his workers. But before planting or harvesting he gives a beer party for his neighbors. Whoever attends sends his wife, or wives, to assist in the work.

Each Kipsigis family lives in a homestead in a village that has an elder knowledgeable in tribal law. He takes serious disputes (such as cattle stealing which, with the practice of sorcery, is the biggest crime a man can commit) to the shire for consideration. Each shire has a leader who not only passes judgment on offenders, but performs ceremonies be-

fore important undertakings and offers prayers to the Kipsigis god, Asis, for his support. The position of shire leader
is hereditary and passes from father to son.

New, modern cement-block square houses, roofed with
iron or corrugated asbestos, rise in Kipsigis territory every
day, but the majority of the people still build traditional
circular huts. They twist strands of wattles between upright
slender poles like a basket, and line the wall with clay and
mud. The floor is of clay also, stamped down firmly and
rubbed with a rounded stone. Before the builders complete
the cone-shaped roof with layers of grass sheafs they build
a platform above the room. This is used for storage, or,
quite often, as sleeping quarters for surplus family members
when the ground floor becomes crowded with goats and
sheep.

The Kipsigis manage with little or no furniture when they
live in the traditional manner. They keep a few large gourds
stoppered with cow tails as milk containers, a large clay pot
for cooking, and animal hides for bedding. They use a slab
of wood or a sheet of hide for the door of a hut, and they
place the doorway facing downhill. If the hut is set on a
plain, it must face east or towards a river. Sometimes a
small shrine stands outside the door where each morning the
Kipsigis make offerings and pray to Asis. They believe that
the power of their one god, which is beneficial only, increases and decreases with the rising and the setting of the
sun.

The Kipsigis build an enclosure near their living quarters
for the cattle. It is called a "boma" and is usually set within
a thornbrush fence as a precaution against predatory ani-

Cattle pass through a village on their way to the stockyards in Mombasa.

mals. By tradition, they say they are "tied to the cows' tails" because from cattle they obtain all nourishing elements.

Kipsigis drink cows' milk from a calabash that has been rubbed with charcoal, and they take blood from a vein in the cow's neck which they cook with vegetables or drink raw. Cows give them flesh, though the Kipsigis refrain from eating meat and drinking milk on the same day. They believe that were they to do so the cows' udders would harden.

One custom that has its roots in the past is that of branding cattle with identifiable nicks in their ears. It is a custom that originated when the Kipsigis were aggressive warriors. After they made surprise attacks upon enemy tribes-people, they would dash in quickly and brand the other fellow's cattle while he was still stunned from the force and unexpectedness of the raid. How this unneighborly attitude has changed! With the new awareness of unity and nationhood, a man with a large herd will lend several head of cattle to his neighbors to be used by them, even to giving him priority over the offspring.

The Kipsigis preserve the reason for their affinity with cattle and other domestic animals in one beautiful legend. Once upon a time sheep, goats, and cattle mingled with wild animals in the deep forests. But one day Asis chose a spot on the edge of a plain where he prepared a tall pyre. He called to the animals to come from their hiding places. When they did so, Asis lit the fire. The leaping flames startled the animals and they fled to safety. However, the cattle, the sheep, and the goats remained, and Asis, pleased with their show of courage, praised and blessed them, and pronounced that from that day they would live with men and provide them with flesh to eat and milk to drink.

When Kenya's new Government introduced the plan for individual farming, the women were at first uncooperative. And they refused to grow corn until experts convinced them that the small yellow corns on the cobs were not their ancestors' teeth as witch doctors had declared them to be. Perhaps the women have benefited the most in the great transition from indiscriminate grazing to systematized, organized crop-farming. They are relieved from lives of drudgery and they share the pleasure of ownership. Women show pride in their fatter cattle, their healthier crops, their plowed lands, and the newer, more efficient tools that are theirs to work with.

5

AGE GROUPS

Many traditions have either disappeared or have been re-adapted to fit the Kenyans' needs of today. Formerly, when a baby was born among the Kipsigis the mother was confined to her hut for three days if the baby was a girl, and four days if it was a boy. To avoid contaminating food, she ate with a stick for six days. To eliminate evil effects, she shaved her head and bathed in the river on the seventh day. Males were banished from her vicinity at the time of the birth, nor were they permitted to look at the baby for one month. The mother weaned her baby when it was one year old; then she fed it wads of *uji*, a kind of porridge made from cornmeal. At times a baby choked and died. Infant mortality in the second year was tragically high—taking almost one-half of all the children born. Generally, death resulted from malnutrition, or pneumonia caused by draughty huts and insufficient clothing, amoebic dysentery, or malaria. Kenya's Government has changed this sad pattern through education. Up-to-date clinics operate through-

Ear-splitting is an unchanging custom among many rural tribes.

out the country, and well-trained district nurses carry their knowledge of hygiene and good-health laws into every home.

Naming a baby was done by rule. The village elder recited the names of the baby's ancestors over and over until the baby sneezed when a particular name was spoken. The parents saw this as an indication that the ancestor's spirit had entered the child.

Some tribes still follow the custom of tying small metal rattles to a child's right wrist. By shaking them and listening to the tinkle of metal against metal the right hand is strengthened. Thus left-handedness, which is considered unlucky, is prevented.

In the harmonious atmosphere of a Kenyan household which is induced by the custom of equal sharing and freely giving, each member carries responsibilities. In country districts, little boys first learn to mind the sheep and goats,

Masai boys and girls of the youngest age group wear ornate jewelry and short hair as do their parents.

then they are promoted to cattle herding. Their sisters watch toddlers and babies, and help with household chores.

In new communities, under the scheme of individual crop-farming, there are many exciting occupations for young people to share. Perhaps the family combines to shuck the corn, or to drive their cattle through the arsenic dip-tank to free them from ticks. Girls like to help pluck the tender young tea leaves, or to roam the fields while they pick white pyrethrum blossoms. They heap the blossoms in carts which the boys trundle to the processing shed. There is an air of purpose and pride in work that they consider pleasure. Of

A Suk warrior from the Northwest accompanies initiation ceremonies on a homemade horn.

course schooling is included in the new system, but that also is accepted as a fine new adventure.

In Kenya education has reached such a high point in importance that it interferes with one age-old custom that will always be observed in most Kenyan tribes. Previously, circumcision schools lasted for at least six months. Now they are held during a school's vacation which does not exceed one month. The age at which a boy attends the school varies, but among the Kipsigis, boys in groups of five enter the circumcision age group between fourteen and eighteen years. They build a special hut in the woods where an elder of their tribe instructs them in the reasons for, and the seriousness of the ritual. The elder, or *Pamongo*, teaches them strict moral codes—that they must not lie or quarrel with another member of the clan; they must love and respect their elders and take pains to use the correct relationship terms. The initiate learns secret rites that form strong links between them and other tribespeople. But the real tests during the course are painful physical ordeals to which the boys must submit to harden their endurance. Should they protest or cry out, they are branded as cowards.

Girls also attend initiation schools, though ones that are less challenging. During the course they are called "Girls of the Bells" because they wear little bells on their wrists.

In the old days, when the classes terminated, boys went on to train as warriors. Unless they return to their studies or to their parents' farms, both boys and girls are now more apt to seek employment, quite often in the towns and cities. They are adults and have entered the marriage-age group.

Although the formalities connected with getting married have slackened among semi-urbanized Kenyans, the practice of *lobola,* or *ruracio*—the bride-price—is the most unshaken of all African customs. With few exceptions, such as among the Kalenjin-speaking Elgeyo people, every prospective

Adolescent girls of the Tharaka-Meru tribe wear leather aprons decorated with colored beads and cowrie shells.

bridegroom in Kenya pays for his bride, either with live-stock or, since Kenya entered a monetary system, with hard cash. In no sense is the young man *buying* his wife. The passing of cattle or money to a girl's parents is a symbol of the permanent welding of two family groups. The cattle and their calves are never eaten or sold. They are merely added to a family's wealth.

The procedures in preparation for a marriage vary among Kenya's diverse people. When a Kipsigis young man announces his intentions, his parents dress in their formal best and call upon the girl's parents. Though the father carries a special stick that clearly indicates the purpose of their visit, the couple wait unannounced so as not to appear too eager. At last the girl's parents come out to greet them, and for a long time the two couples exchange pleasantries. Finally, the boy's parents introduce the matter that is foremost in everyone's mind. They discuss the possibility of marriage between their offspring. It is important to determine that the families are not related, even distantly, for a powerful taboo exists pertaining to blood ties.

On subsequent visits the four parents decide on the bride-price, which among Kipsigis who live in the back country is eight cows and twenty-three goats. Negotiations conclude when the girl's parents make a symbolic gesture by anointing the foreheads of the boy's parents with butter.

Gifts are freely exchanged between the two families until the day of the wedding. The bridegroom sends an emissary with two children to fetch his bride. She arrives carrying a calabash filled with sour milk, symbolizing fertility, and the couple exchange grass-woven bracelets called *sequtiets*.

The bridegroom's family prepares an elaborate feast which the relatives of both clans share. Singing and dancing and much laughter continue for several days before the newly married couple settle into life under the guidance of the boy's parents. A wedding everywhere is a joyful occasion, but in Kenya it is doubly so, for it is the permanent uniting of two clans.

Modern conditions complicate the ancient custom. When a young man leaves his family to work in a town he does not always have his father's support in providing the lobola cattle. He must find the bride-price himself, and it is almost always cash. The price is high, especially when he wants to marry a girl from an alien tribe. It can reach $1,500, a very

These Boran dancers belong to the Galla tribe, which migrated to Kenya from Ethiopia.

inflated figure in proportion to his earnings which, annually, can be less than one-third of the bride-price. Young couples work together in order to pay the debt. But a girl is happy. A marriage that has been so dearly bought is more likely to endure.

And the Kenya government is satisfied that lobola is a tradition that is well worth preserving. Despite present conflicting opinions in Kenya—that the price should be stabilized, or remain flexible as it is today, or that it should be abolished for it tends to make old men avaricious and keeps young men poor—no doubt the Government will provide a solution that will retain so dignified and noble an institution as the custom of the bride-price.

6

SINCE THE TURN
OF THE CENTURY

Kenya's modern history started in 1901 when the British completed the building of the railroad from Mombasa to Lake Victoria. Prior to the launching of the hazardous venture (five years earlier), incursions by Europeans beyond the coastline were infrequent. The railroad established the first permanent contact between Kenyans and Europeans. A year later the influx of settlers began.

Britain's motives for undertaking the prodigious task of installing a railroad across unknown wild country were threefold. An altruistic motive was a sincere desire to put down the cruel slave traffic that rampaged along Lake Victoria's western shore. A second motive for building a railroad was that it seemed a practical means of opening the territory for exploitation. A third strong motive was political. The Germans, to strengthen their grip on African territory, were nosing a railroad into German East Africa to the south of Kenya in what is now the Republic of Tanzania.

Would the British have attempted the colossal undertaking had they known the tremendous expenditure in energy, personal comfort, and money that lay ahead? The average cost of the construction, including the erection of bridges, viaducts, and all the trappings pertaining to railroads, was reckoned to be about $30,000 for every tortuous mile. This is a trivial figure compared to the 25,259 casualties that resulted in the loss of 2,493 lives and 6,454 permanently disabled persons.

The British brought 35,733 Hindus from India when they failed to enlist Africans for the job. From the start, almost insurmountable problems and dilemmas faced engineers and working crew. The reports of droughts, famine, floods, landslides, locust plagues, unfamiliar diseases, epidemics, insubordinations, termites that ate the wooden ties, hostile natives who shot with poisoned arrows, natives who stole equipment, and a host of other dreadful calamities that they experienced inspired writers to produce a mountain of books, lectures, and a Hollywood movie. One exciting incident was the overturning of a locomotive by a rhinoceros, but the episode of the two man-eating lions of Tsavo created the greatest furor of all.

Night after terror-filled night the lions, old and maneless but conniving and sly, raided the camp and carried off a victim. Traps were set and poisoned bait was laid but the wily beasts ignored them. Night after night snipers waited in the trees and listened to the earth-shaking roars coming closer.

They heard the screams from victims as the lions carried them away, the crunch of bones as the lions gorged. The animals eluded the watching snipers for many months. The courage and tenacity of a young English engineer, J. H. Patterson, brought the brutes to their deserved ends. He stalked the lions at great peril to himself and finally bagged one. But a further eighteen months passed before he shot its mate. The jubilant workers hailed Colonel Patterson as their hero—their deliverer. A few days later they presented him with an inscribed silver bowl and a long poem written in the Hindustani language by one talented workman.

Colonel Patterson also wrote a book, *The Man-Eaters of Tsavo*, which makes stirring and exciting reading even after sixty years. What became of the lions? They were mounted and sent to the Field Museum of Natural History in Chicago where they are still on exhibit.

Kenya and Uganda were claimed as Protectorates of British East Africa by the time trade had opened in the vicinity of Lake Victoria. Elephant tusks were the biggest marketable item, though small amounts of hides and skins, wild rubber, and beeswax also rolled by rail over the 520 miles to the coast. However, income from the export of these items was insufficient to pay for the expensive railroad. The train passed beautiful high, open, seemingly unoccupied country en route. It was ideal farmland for producing crops and cattle, suitable for export to Europe where people were always hungry. And if emigrants could be persuaded to farm in Kenya, England would be relieved of her surplus population. Thus started the occupation of land with a view of Mount Kenya by European farmers.

People living near Lake Victoria or along the Indian Ocean were virtually untouched by British settlement. But white farmers who bought land on the highlands unwittingly blocked nomadic herdsmen's expansion into country that, though empty of humans, was theirs by honorable, tribal ownership. The Kenyans were robbed of their ancestral homes, the very foundations of their culture. This terrible mistake was the basis for future sizzling discord and explosive events. Although settlers had paid for the land, the Kikuyu and Kipsigis tribes thought that the payment was for transitory use only.

Authorities on Kenyan Native law such as Dr. L. S. B. Leakey, an ordained elder of the Kikuyu tribes, believe that drought and famine, a smallpox epidemic, a rinderpest scourge that had decimated the cattle, a locust plague, and a war between the Kikuyu and the Masai tribes had temporarily emptied the land prior to English settlement. The tribespeople, herding their cattle before them, would have in time come back.

The British Colonial Office in London set up a sytsem of government in Kenya. Younger men administered the law from Native Councils in remote outposts. They reported to District Commissioners whose duties were to see that justice was done, taxes paid, disputes settled, famine and disease controlled, and laws obeyed. The District Commissioners reported to a governor in Nairobi from whom they received instructions that originated in London. Under the system the British were unquestionably the masters, the Kenyans were the subordinates. The settlers on what came to be called the White Highlands built a thriving community

A view of the White Highlands from the Aberdare Mountain range.

through perseverance and initiative, though at times they suffered frustrations because of a lack of cooperation, and often failure due to their inexperience. But the settlers' occupation of the land aroused intangible, psychological problems that ate like cankers into the souls of the humiliated Kenyans. Though District Commissioners placed great stress on justice and the settlers looked after material comforts with good food, housing, and medical care—often administered at great inconvenience to themselves—on the whole, neither the commissioners nor the settlers persevered in understanding the complex laws observed by the proud Kenyans who lived in the vicinity of the highlands.

A high density population in some areas sparked a land dispute that grew to gigantic proportions. Formerly, a Kenyan farmer expanded his property as his family of sons increased. Additional land was a provision for their future as independent farmers while still being accepted as members of the family. But European fences barred expansion. Kenyans living under crowded conditions regarded the wide acres of land, seemingly unoccupied except for fat Hereford cattle, with resentment. They had not yet learned that cultivated lands produce richer crops and better cattle.

Not all Kenyans resented the coming of the British. There were many strong and enduring loyalties built between the black and white peoples of Kenya. As evidence of their support, 20,000 Kenyans volunteered for active service in German East Africa during the First World War (1914-1918). Their assistance helped to bring about the defeat of their common enemy, Germany. (In World War II, Kenyan regiments helped to oust the Italians, Britain's antagonists, in Somaliland and Ethopia.)

But as British administrators became more firmly entrenched and the land was proclaimed the Kenya Colony and Protectorate in 1920, tensions increased and the attitude of blacks towards whites became more openly hostile. In 1934 a delegation from London analyzed land distribution in Kenya. Although the delegates reported that white settlers had actually alienated only 106¾ square miles out of a total of 16,000 square miles on the highlands, most Africans refused to accept the figure. Rumbles of discontent continued. The rumble became a roar. Protests at last found expression in the shocking Kikuyu Mau Mau rebellion that started in 1952. It was the first organized revolt against European occupation of East Africa.

Basically, Mau Mau was as much a religious uprising as it was political and in a desperate effort to evict Christian doctrines while protesting the loss of land, Mau Mau members reverted to savage practices belonging to their own primitive, pagan past. New Mau Mau members were forced to take oaths of a diabolical, obscene nature and to swear that they would murder every European with whom they had contact. Lonely families on isolated farms were haunted constantly with a fear of the unexpected. The quiet footfall in the dead of night could be a vengeful prowler come to slay them—or destroy their pedigreed cattle—or to fire their homes. Their employees, though benign in behavior, could have concealed about their persons pangas as sharp as razors. Nor were Africans loyal to the British spared. They went about their duties in constant dread, for they, too, were subjected to barbarous punishments if their Mau Mau masters suspected them of disobedience. Ironically, the Mau Mau uprising injured more black Kenyans, morally and physically, than it did the whites.

The British administrators declared a state of Emergency. Patrols of British troops made sorties into the deep forests and routed bands of Mau Mau from their hiding places. They arrested thousands of suspects whom they retained in work camps without trial because of the Emergency. In rehabilitation centers they resorted to de-oathing ceremonies which were conducted by loyalist witch doctors. It was tragic indeed for the hundreds of innocent Africans who paid the ultimate penalty along with the guilty in the confusion of mopping up the terrorists. And during the Emergency period, as compensation for past negligence, the British stepped up land development and other benefits in African areas, such as the Machakos scheme.

Among the Mau Mau leaders who were tried and sentenced to either imprisonment or death was Jomo Kenyatta, Kenya's President, who was sentenced to a seven-year prison term. Some years earlier Kenyatta had asked for and had been granted permission to operate a school system throughout the Kikuyu territory on the slopes of Mount Kenya. Perhaps so desperate a situation called for a desperate remedy, but it was behind the innocent facade of small country schools that Mau Mau propaganda was nurtured and from them it spread.

Jomo Kenyatta.

When loyalist Africans were questioned as to the reasons for the uprising, they invariably answered that it was an accumulation of problems and irritations that could only be solved by force, the chief problem being discrimination in almost every black-white relationship—from employment to education to social contacts. The British Government saw that a return to the previous mode of life with white colonials completely dominating subservient black Africans would result in a repetition of a building up of similar tensions. It wisely gave the Kenyans widespread voting powers despite the objections of some embittered white highlanders.

During the Emergency, the spirit of independence had flashed east from Ghana, the first freed colonial country south of the Sahara. *Uhuru*, the swahili word for "Freedom," was contagious, and the Mau Mau bloodbath in Kenya had served to spur the pace for independence. Aspirants for *Uhuru sasa*, which means "Freedom now," put pressure on the Government for permission to form political parties. The permission was granted on a district basis only (not nationwide). Because of the Emergency, however, adult Kenyans were made to take a Loyalty Oath to the British Government before they were eligible to vote.

In 1957, the first Kenya elections for representation in the Legislative Council were held and eight African elected members were admitted to the Council. A second election in 1959 advanced African elected members of the Legislative Council from eight to fourteen. By 1960, the Council had an African majority with thirty-three of the fifty-three constituency seats. During the same year the British ended the state of Emergency. It had cost them $150,000,000 to crush the revolt.

Meanwhile, pressure for the release of Jomo Kenyatta by the Kenya African National Union (KANU)—the successor to Mr. Kenyatta's banned party, the Kenya African Union— had increased through 1959 and 1960. But it was not until August, 1961, that he emerged from detention.

Faithful followers waited for Kenyatta, stoutly denying the charges that had been made against him. Kenyatta strode through the country, whipping the people into a frenzy with forceful speeches advocating freedom. *"Uhuru!"* he shouted to them, and *"Harambee!"* a new slogan, which, roughly, means "Let's all pull together." And the excited crowds thundered back to him, *"Uhuru! Uhuru na Kenyatta!"*

At one rally in Nakuru, Kenyatta spoke before 350 European farmers. "We want you to stay and farm in our country," he declared. "This is the policy of the Government."

As strong proof of the persuasive qualities and magnetism of this great statesman who does not waste his energies in bitter recrimination, the audience responded with shouts of *"Harambee!"* Though Kenyatta was partly responsible for the uncertainties, the fears, the horrors of the 1950's, there are few Europeans who do not hold an affection for him, who do not speak of him with respect.

Mr. Kenyatta pressed for self-government, and Kenyans continued to gain political strength. After a series of amicable constitutional discussions, the British Government yielded and on June 1, 1963, Kenyans attained self-government and prepared to take over the ruling of their country. However, though now free of interference by foreign powers, they still owed allegiance to Britain's Queen Elizabeth II.

December 11, 1963, was the date set for formal recognition of Kenya's new status. Heads of states and dignitaries from many world nations converged in Nairobi. There were Kenyan citizens there also, in the hundreds of thousands. They came from the shores of Lake Victoria and the palm-fringed sandy beaches of the Indian Ocean, from the green slopes of Mount Kenya and the stark deserts of the northeast. Their goal was the new Independence Stadium, there to witness Jomo Kenyatta taking the oath as Kenya's Prime Minister. On the stroke of midnight the lights went out, and in the velvet dark of a Kenya night Britain's flag was lowered. A pause—then on came the lights to show Kenya's new black, red, and green flag floating from the pole's top. A great triumphant shout burst from the throats of blacks, whites, Asians, Arabs. "*Uhuru na Umoja*," the people shouted. "Freedom and Unity!" Kenya was the thirty-fifth African country to reach the glorious state of independence.

Kenyans then expressed their wish for full independence by becoming a Republic, though they requested that their country be included in the British Commonwealth of Nations. Other Commonwealth members consented to Kenya's application for membership, so on December 12, 1964, Kenya became a Republic within the British Commonwealth of Nations with Jomo Kenyatta unanimously acclaimed the country's first President.

7

UHURU NA UMOJA

Uhuru meant many things to the varied races that comprise the Kenyan people. To small farmers it meant pride in ownership, to office workers it meant higher pay and a chance for promotion, to students it meant better schools and scholarships. To Kenyan women, Uhuru held the promise of freedom from drudging lives, of being transformed from nonentities into individuals, recognized for their dependability, their true loyalty in the cause of nationalism. But for other thousands of Kenyans, Uhuru was a large and ominous question mark. To Hindus, Moslems, Sikhs, Europeans, and workers for Europeans, the future looked bleak indeed. They felt themselves to be captives of circumstances. Where could they go—how could they reorganize their disrupted lives!

Retired Europeans who had spent all their lives in Kenya and who were too old to start again were particularly saddened with their prospects. Oversensitive Europeans saw destitution ahead for their employees, and with heavy hearts set about finding alternative work for them in a rapidly contracting labor market.

As far back as April, 1963, the *East African Standard* suggested in one article: "The promises of benefits to come after Uhuru are so glittering that KANU courts the risk of bitter blame if the realities break faith."

Pessimists had underestimated Jomo Kenyatta's administrative abilities and had forgotten that some years earlier his Russian teacher, Bronislav Malinowski, had described him as "combining a knowledge of Western manners and Western modes of thought with an essentially African education and way of looking at things."

Jomo Kenyatta set about placating the fears of all people, on every side. He asked alien residents to remain in the country (providing they took out Kenyan citizenship) and to share in the promised benefits that were yet to come. Although about 40 percent of the British farmers sold their properties (for cash loaned by the British Government to Kenya), the remainder chose to stay. Many Indians moved to England or back to India; the problems of other misplaced persons still await solutions.

To Africans, Kenyatta delivered his opinions on tribalism like strong drumbeats on a hollowed log. "Beware of negative, belligerent tribalism that sees no good in an alien tribe," he cautioned. "It must go! Forget that your origin is Kikuyu, Kipsigis, Suk, Luo or of any other tribe. Substitute your tribalism with mass nationalism—Unity!" He repeated such injunctions over and over again. Though Kenyans now had freedom—Uhuru—they must practice Freedom *and* Unity

—*Uhuru na Umoja*. By such commands Kenyatta succeeded in welding his people into one powerful national force, making Kenya the most stable new nation in Africa.

Kenyatta's life prior to his emergence from detention is as dramatic as his performance in the role of President. His age is indefinite, but possibly he is in his late seventies. He was born to Kikuyu farmer parents, but in 1903 he ran away from home. He found shelter in a Church of Scotland mission where he received schooling and treatment for a spinal disease. When he had recovered from his illness, Kenyatta, whose name at that time was Kamau wa Ngengi, learned carpentry when he could spare time from his duties in the mission's kitchen. Later, he worked as an inspector of water supplies in Nairobi. It was there that he changed his name.

Kenyatta was drawn to politics during the 1920's, and became general secretary of a political party, the Kikuyu Central Association. He also published a Kikuyu language newspaper in which he built up the case against British occupation of Kenya's highlands. In 1929, he was one of a delegation to sail for England to protest British domination in Kenya.

Two years later Kenyatta took up residence in England. During his fifteen years away from Kenya, Kenyatta completed a postgraduate course in anthropology, visited Russia on three occasions (on one visit enrolling in the Lenin School of Subversion), appeared in a movie with Paul Robeson (the American Negro singer with whom he shared an apartment together with Peter Abraham, the South African writer), and wrote an important book called *Facing Mount Kenya*. The book created a sensation because in it Kenyatta placed the blame on the methods missionaries used in teaching (though not always practicing) Christianity for the confused thinking and frustrations of many Africans.

Although married to an English girl by whom he had a son, Kenyatta abandoned both wife and son in 1943 and went back to Kenya. He was caught in a gripping desire for his country's freedom and saw clearly what action he must take.

As president of the Kenya African Union party (KAU), and represented in Kenya's Parliament, he called again and again for Kenya's independence. Then the Mau Mau uprising began, KAU was banned, Jomo Kenyatta was tried, served his term in prison, and was released. That brings Kenyatta's

The Parliament Buildings in Nairobi.

story back to the present, with him as President of the Republic of Kenya.

Kenya's President is also Commander-in-Chief of the
Armed Forces. He is normally elected at the General Election which follows the dissolution of Parliament occurring
every five years. The presidential candidate who receives
the support of the majority of elected members of Parliament
wins the presidency.

Kenya's President, a Vice-President, and a cabinet of
twenty ministers determine the policies of their country.
They follow a one-party system under KANU, the government party, and they call it African Socialism.

African Socialism follows a policy that adheres to the
Kenyan traditions of political equality and mutual social
responsibility. Political rights offer the individual an opportunity to participate in political activities as an equal, having
to prove nothing beyond age, citizenship, and allegiance to
his country. As a participating equal in government affairs
the individual can exercise his ambitions, whether he is working on the land, or in industry, or in trade. The policy is in
line with African tradition that heeds the opinion of every
man in village meetings held under a Council of Chiefs.

Social responsibility, as put into practice by African Socialism, is a direct extension of *Ujamaa* (meaning "Family-
hood"), which has been through the ages the binding factor
of Kenyan tribal life. African Socialism extends beyond the
family and tribe, and a true African Socialist considers all
Kenyans as his brothers—as members of his ever-extending
family. As a member of one great society, the individual has
a responsibility for his fellow citizens, and to do his best for

A Meru chief from the eastern slopes of Mt. Kenya.

them with the knowledge that if society prospers so will he share in that prosperity which will come only with the full cooperation of each member.

Mr. Kenyatta stresses two points—that African Socialism differs from Communism because it insures every mature citizen equal political rights, and that it differs from Western capitalism because it prevents economic power groups from exercising political pressures.

African Socialism welcomes foreign investors, but with certain limitations to forestall their domination. Investors who bring capital into Kenya must be prepared to accept the spirit of mutual social responsibility. They must make shares in their companies available to Kenyans who wish to

The residential buildings near Nairobi of the Kenya Institute of Administration.

buy them, and who will, perhaps, as their earning powers increase, buy *all* the shares of foreign companies. Foreign investors must provide training facilities for their African employees and employ them at executive levels as soon as they are qualified.

Despite the restrictions imposed upon it, foreign business, particularly that of America, had increased investments from $57 million two years earlier to well over $100 million by 1967. In 1964, twenty American companies had businesses in Kenya; in 1967, there were sixty-two. There are still Indian and British interests in Nairobi, but they are now outnumbered by American interests. Two American advertising agencies maintain offices, and two American airlines have each invested in a new, big hotel. Soap manufacturing companies operate plants, sewing machine companies assemble their machines in Kenya, and fruits and juices are canned under American labels. Such is America's faith in Kenya's future under African Socialism.

President Kenyatta also has faith in a system that lets a man hold his head high with the pride that comes with social equality and the knowledge that he is one of a large, mutually working-together family. Kenyatta likes African Socialism, but he holds contempt for Western capitalism, and he abhors Communism—any kind, either Russian or Chinese. In 1965, he expelled journalists who promoted Soviet views and causes, and he closed the Lumumba Institute in Nairobi for the same reason.

Yet Chinese Communism is blatantly flaunted just across Kenya's borders—to the south, the west, and the east. Early in 1965, the Chinese succeeded in establishing a sort of beachhead in Tanzania. Red Chinese agents trained insurgents for use against Tshombe's Katanga Government in the Congo. They supported the Congolese rebels, rampant at the time, because they saw the prospects for revolution all over Africa. In Mao-Tse Tung's words, "If we can take the Congo we shall hold the whole of Africa."

The Chinese broadcast revolutionary propaganda one hundred hours weekly towards Africa in a half dozen languages, including Swahili. To curry favor they gave a clinic to Zanzibar, large bribes to subversives, and a pledge of $41.6 million as aid to Tanzania. From Dar-es-Salaam, Tanzania's capital, the Chinese Communists shipped arms for use by the rebels, either by rail to the shores of Lake Tanganyika, or by air to Arua, a main distributing point in Uganda.

President Kenyatta warned Peking against interference in

Kenya's internal affairs when reports reached him of Chinese bribes to opposition groups. But in May, 1965, the Communists brazenly sent a convoy of eleven trucks across Kenya's Nyanza Province. Kenyatta seized the trucks (operated by the Uganda Army), arrested their twenty-seven escorts for smuggling, and confiscated seventy-five tons of Red Chinese weapons.

The ensuing turmoil revealed the traitorous activities of Kenya's Vice-President, Oginga Odinga, who bragged that "Communism is like food to me" and who admitted having accepted hundreds of thousands of dollars from various Communist capitals. Odinga's powers were gradually whittled until in March, 1966, he resigned. For a time Kenya faced the possibility of serious disruption in the Harambee program when Odinga formed a new opposition party, the

President Kenyatta with the presidents of other new African nations—Milton Obote of Uganda (left), Kenneth Kaunda of Zambia (right).

Kenya's People Union (KPU). Though KPU won nine of twenty-seven seats contested during the "Little General Election" held in June, 1966, it was no threat to the Government's KANU which has 150 Parliament seats plus twelve specially elected members.

To further the cause of Chinese Communism in East Africa, Peking remedied the budget deficit in Somalia, the desert nation to Kenya's east. Until October, 1967, Somalia caused bigger headaches to the new Kenyan Government than impressing the importance of Harambee and Uhuru na Umoja on Kenya's citizens. During that month opposing forces reached a compromise.

About 200,000 wandering Somalis scratch a meager living from the hot, arid northeast wastelands. At the time of independence they emphatically expressed a wish to join the

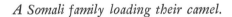

A Somali family loading their camel.

Somalia Republic. But they did not move and they refused to live as Kenyan citizens. The Somalia Government argued that its country's boundary should be pushed westward to include them (almost one-third of Kenyan land), for ethnically it was reasonable that the Hamitic expatriates should be incorporated into their own homeland. But President Kenyatta was adamant in preserving the "solemn decision that all African states shall adhere to the boundaries inherited at independence."

The Somalia Government turned a blind eye on hordes of Somali *shiftas* (a Swahili word meaning "bandit" or "brigand") when they raided Kenyan Army and police posts, government offices and food stores. The tall, arrogant, sinewy, coffee-colored shiftas attacked with the persistence of wounded buffaloes, accounting for three thousand deaths over a four-year period. Security operations were costing the Kenya Government $8.4 million a year and President Kenyatta's patience was wearing thin. When the shiftas started planting land bombs along the roads in 1966, he resorted to the same tactics the British had used in rounding up the Mau Mau terrorists. He herded the nomadic Somalis into fortified villages. There they were registered, given grazing permits, but were forced to come home at night. Now, fourteen such villages support 80 percent of the Somalis who live in Kenya.

In June, 1967, a Somali delegation from the villages called on Mr. Kenyatta in Nairobi and repeated their confidence in the Kenyan Government and their loyalty to Kenya. They said that they were persuading shiftas to surrender their arms. Relations between Kenya and Somalia continue to improve.

In late October, 1967, at a meeting under the chairmanship of President Kenneth Kaunda of Zambia in Arusha, Tanzania, a resolution was signed by President Kenyatta and Mr. Mohammed Haji Ibrahim Egal, Prime Minister of Somalia. They agreed to maintain peace on both sides of the border by preventing the destruction of life and property and to refrain from conducting hostile propaganda such as by radio and the press. Instead, they agreed to promote the development of friendly relations and to reopen diplomatic relations between the two countries. To prevent future friction, a working committee consisting of Somalia, Kenya, and Zambia will meet periodically to examine ways and means of bringing about a lasting solution to major and minor differences between Somalia and Kenya.

The Somalis who make Kenya their home will welcome a permanent peace, for they appreciate the benefits that a well-organized Development Plan brings to them.

Kenya's Minister of Economic Planning and Development, the Hon. Mr. T. J. Mboya, formed a five-year Development Plan to cover the years 1964-1970 (it was revised in 1966) that embraces every facet of life in Kenya—its land and agriculture, industry, education, health, welfare, and the conservation of the country's wildlife. Because agriculture is Kenya's most significant national asset, it receives prior consideration in Kenya's road towards complete Uhuru na Umoja.

8

HARAMBEE
AT WORK

After four years of independence, President Kenyatta's oft-repeated "Back to the Land" call brought the first fruits of freedom harvests to the small Kenyan farmer despite a serious drought in 1965.

Through the centuries it had been the custom for each rural family to grow little more than sufficient for its own use. The small surplus, perhaps of corn, mangoes, bananas, was displayed for sale in the nearest village market. The precious cattle were seldom disposed of, but grazed contentedly wherever they chose, trampling the land and causing irreparable erosion. The traditional pattern is changing rapidly.

Three-quarters of Kenya's people derive their living from subsistence agriculture, and the products of the land are Kenya's biggest single economic asset. Under the Develop-

President Kenyatta with Dr. Chidzero, the new Resident Representative, at the opening of the Nairobi office of the United Nations Technical Assistance Board.

ment Plan, the Government lends money to individual farmers to buy better seed, improved stock, fertilizers, and machinery. Its experts give advice on how to produce superior crops that are suitable for marketing on a national scale. As Mr. Kenyatta stated at the opening of Parliament on February 15, 1967, "The land is the place where the ordinary man and woman can do most to build the nation. When one farmer increases his cultivations and improves his farm by harder work, it is a personal achievement. When ten thousand farmers follow his example, it becomes a national achievement."

A farmer who holds the title to his land has the security

to invest in improvements. He can use his land as collateral for loans to help raise production upon the advice of government extension officers. In 1965, the Government loaned $18 million to farmers. By 1970, the figure is expected to increase to $50 million as roads are improved and new ones built, better marketing facilities are established, and more farmers increase their output. Already, 250,000 small farmers maintain coffee and tea plantations—entirely new ventures for them.

Cooperatives in the Development Plan enable small farmers to make a real contribution to the economy of their country. Under the system there are three main types of farms. Some farmers cultivate their own land but market their products collectively, others own their land but combine in working it and sharing implements such as harvesters and tractors. Bigger farms are owned and worked communally.

Prior to independence, crops for export such as coffee, tea, pyrethrum, cotton, sisal, tobacco, were cultivated on the large "white" farms. Since the departure of many European farmers their lands have been made available to Kenyans for purchase on easy terms (up to 80 percent) over a long period. The Government tries to keep the big farms intact in the interests of high quality production. In several instances Kenyans have ventured as partners in big farm operation, but on the whole the "white highlands" estates have been carved into segments suitable for small farms. Imported deciduous trees that lined long avenues have been razed and spacious lawns plowed under. The European houses have fallen into disrepair and will eventually crumble under vigorous African growth that always, given time, claims everything that is alien. The 60 percent of European farmers who still work farms in Kenya have the repeated assurance of President Kenyatta that they are welcome. "We need them more than we realized," he has been heard to declare. It is on the highly mechanized European farms that, even today, the bulk of Kenya's exportable agricultural products are cultivated.

Kenya's Development Plan includes the preparation of one million acres of semi-arid lands on which 75,000 farming families will be settled by 1970. The settlements are scattered throughout the country, but one fine example is located in Shimba Hills, thirty miles to the south of Mombasa. Formerly the area was the abode of lions, elephants,

An experimental farm in Shimba Hills.

and tsetse flies; now it is an integrated community where farmers from different tribes live and work in the spirit of Harambee. They have turned deserts into gardens by hard work and cooperation.

At first it was not easy to persuade farmers to settle in such ill-reputed land as Shimba Hills, now every plot is allotted. New settlers build their own houses with free materials and transport. One farmer, Mr. Muiya Muoka, an ex-soldier, typifies the Shimba Hills farmer. He was one of the first settlers, and in true pioneer spirit he overcame many difficulties when others were defeated and abandoned their projects. He not only runs a successful farm, but he and a staff also work as contractors for the Government; with three tractors, a transport truck, and a Land-Rover, they plow and harrow for their neighbors. Mr. Muoka has repaid one development loan and is now repaying a second.

A cooperative society handles the produce from corn, sorghums, bananas, and cassava, and it mills the sugarcane. River and spring water irrigates tobacco and sisal fields, cashew nuts, coconut, and citrus orchards in Shimba Hills. Farmers pay small fees for compulsory cattle-dipping to get rid of the ticks, and for curative drugs to combat trypanosomiasis which afflicts cattle wherever there are tsetse flies. Almost everything else is free. The Government provides a medical clinic, agricultural seminars, four grade schools and three nursery schools. On a self-help basis, settlers have added four grade schools to this number, and they give one day each week to constructing roads, bridges, and other projects towards development. Shimba Hills serves as a model of applied farming by diligent farmers.

A cooperative group digging a trench.

Kenyan farmers are active in every field of agriculture—from dairy farming to ranching. One prosperous innovation was started by Mr. Samuel Mariga on the Ngorika Settlement Scheme which was formerly a large European estate. Mr. Mariga's red, ripe, flavorsome strawberries are served at the best hotels in Europe. He works along with sixty employees. They tend the plants, pick the berries, and pack them in attractive containers lined with green tissue paper. The berries speed by truck to the Horticulture Cooperative Union in Nairobi which sees that they are air-freighted and served almost before the dew on them dries. Mr. Mariga also grows tomatoes, peppers, peas, and beans for export. For domestic consumption he raises sheep and dairy cows.

Harambee at work is most active on the 203-acre Wambugu Farm which the late Senior Chief Wambugu leased to

Planting strawberries on the Mariga farm.

the County Council for training farmers in modern, mechanized methods. Courses that cover every branch of farming are given to an average of one thousand ambitious farmers every year.

The Farmers' Training College at Thomson's Falls (about thirty-seven miles northeast of Nakuru) provides instruction in large-scale farming to men who bought properties up to six hundred acres from Europeans on a willing-seller, willing-buyer basis. The British Government provided the initial capital to run the college and shared the recurrent expenditures, first with the Kenyan Government and, since 1966, with the Norwegian Government.

The college places emphasis on practical farming rather than on theoretical. As the college's principal says, "The idea is to produce farmers who can actually do the work in the field and not just sit on the porch."

Trainees learn the basic skills connected with large-scale

farming—from farm bookkeeping to agricultural economics, from dairy management to animal husbandry. In carpentry classes they learn to build everything that requires wood—from chicken coops to pig pens.

Since one aim of the Development Plan is to bring higher incomes to the people, it also directs its energies towards other occupations. The expansion of Kenya's fisheries receives the attention of the Plan. By stocking Lakes Rudolph and Baringo, and by using modernized fishing methods on them and on Lake Victoria, by 1970 the annual output is expected to treble—from 20,000 tons to 60,000.

Products of the land and water are not enough to assure Kenya's progress. The Plan also includes industrial development. It protects while it encourages foreign enterprises

A typical native bull calf on an experimental farm.

under the terms of a Foreign Investment Act, and it helps the thousands of Kenyan citizens who have gone into business, either wholesale or retail, with small loans from either the Development Finance Company of Kenya (DFCK) or the Industrial and Commercial Development Corporation. DFCK examined twenty-five new projects before investing part of the required capital to operate them. The Ministry of Commerce and Industry invented a striking new slogan, "Build Kenya, buy Kenyan," which alerted the public and opened the businesses of smaller manufacturers and merchants to eager consumers.

The entrance to the Migori gold mine, Nyanza Province.

A wide variety of articles come from small factories—to be sold in small shops. Whether the manufacturer makes baby foods or ball-point pens, metal or plastic ware, house paint or paint brushes, he works in the spirit of Harambee for he knows he is helping Kenya's economy and easing unemployment.

Among the major projects are cotton mills that produce beautiful patterned dress lengths for women, and woollen mills that make soft, warm blankets for use against the cold of Kenya's highlands. The East African Oil Refinery on the coast processes 6,000 gallons of crude oil daily, from which it makes fuel oil for locomotives and jet aircraft. The refinery also processes gasoline, bunker oil, and bitumen.

The Tana River Development Company's objective is to develop the hydroelectric power resources of the Tana River. It was started in 1964 and will be an important contribution to industrial development when it is finished. The work progresses in stages as the demand for electricity grows. The ultimate installed capacity will be 300 megawatts, and by looking far into the future, the scheme is envisaged as providing sufficient power to meet all of Kenya's needs for many years to come.

In every way, Harambee—"Let's All Pull Together"—has brought a better, a more fruitful, and richer life to Kenya's people. Mr. Kenyatta was justifiably proud of his country's progress when in 1967 he assessed the achievements. "We have won through a phase of patient planning, based on the principle of our African Socialism," said the President.

9

THE YEARNING
FOR LEARNING

In Kenya's early days the rugged, jungled mountains were classrooms that exposed to young Kenyan eyes visions of the natural life of which they were so thoroughly a part. To sharp Kenyan ears they gave the sounds that alerted them to danger. Kenyans had no need for books and schools, though the learning imposed upon them called for great toil and exertion—as equally great as sitting in a formal classroom. To learn to identify a stealthy carnivoral footfall took concentration, and to learn the warning telltale caws of gray louri birds required as close attention, for instance, as young Americans memorizing in their proper sequence the names of all our Presidents.

The gruelling examinations to which young Kenyans submitted were as rigid as senior high-school tests elsewhere, but the young adults emerged from the ordeals strong, fearless, and capable of defending the clan against their most potent enemies.

As soon as the railroad from Mombasa to Kisumu was completed, missionaries opened the doors to book learning in Kenya. They built one-room schools of mud and clay and roofed them with grass sheaves. But it was hard to lure young people who belonged to the wild open places. By exercising patience and using material inducements such as food and clothing, the missionaries succeeded in establishing an education system, though they rarely extended their teaching beyond grade-school level. When the British colonized Kenya its Government took over the financing of the small missionary schools.

As the Western way of life intruded more and more into the traditional Kenya it caused disruptions in the age-old system. The Kenyans were quick to recognize that the meager education given to them by missionary schools and the scarcity of higher education were insufficient to meet the Europeans on an equal footing, nor was it sufficient to qualify them to compete for a share in the good things Europeans introduced. They could be set free, and progress, only by education. Kenyans saw that next in importance to Uhuru, when it came, was a need for general education without which Uhuru could not be permanently maintained. A passionate clamor for learning commenced and the new Harambee Government acted.

During the four years following independence, Kenya's high-school enrollment swelled until it doubled to 50,000 students in the country's 400 new secondary schools. The number of students attending 5,100 simple one-story cement grade schools increased from 900,000 to well over one million during the same period. Not only had every child been given the *wish* to learn but also the facilities wherein to learn.

Integrated educational institutions operate on all levels in Kenya. Several technical high schools and two trade schools have full-capacity enrollments. The most advanced of the technical schools are the Kenya Polytechnic (with 1,500 students) and the Mombasa Technical Institute. The University College in Nairobi was established in 1954. It is a constituent college of the new University of East Africa, along with the University Colleges of Makerere (Uganda) and Dar-es-Salaam (Tanzania). The college has faculties of

Students in an automobile workshop they built.

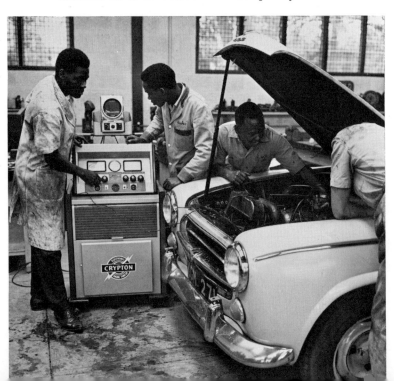

Students of a land-surveying course.

the Arts, Science, Architecture, and Veterinary Sciences. The majority of the professors and instructors of the University College are Africans and they lecture to about 1,200 enrolled students of which less than 200 are women.

The University College offers extracurricular activities that are of a strictly interracial nature. Students have a wide choice, from religious clubs to outdoor mountain-climbing clubs, and debating societies that discuss topics which may include the value of the bride-price or the political problems of less successful new African nations. A writers' workshop within the college publishes an excellent literary magazine, *Nexus*, to which many promising journalist students contribute.

A geo-chemistry survey team gathering mineral samples in South Nyanza to be sent to Nairobi for analysis.

The first multiracial, multitribal advanced secondary school in Kenya is Strathmore Boarding College (or Prep School) for boys. It is under the sponsorship of Opus Dei, an international association of Roman Catholic laymen. The Kenyan Government gave a capital grant towards the construction of the buildings and it bears some of the operating costs. Philanthropic groups contribute towards the school's maintenance, including the Ford Foundation, which gave seventy-five scholarships over a three-year period. Mr. David C. Sperling, an American from Connecticut, was the first principal of the school, which opened in March, 1961, with an enrollment of sixty boys. Today, Strathmore's capacity is 120 boys who study academic courses as well as elective courses such as languages, world affairs, and sociology. Senior students take the Advanced General Certificate of Education (a test that is flown from England and then flown back for correction), or the entrance examinations to East African universities. Strathmore College is Harambee at work, for students together see nation-building as their dedicated duty.

During 1967, teacher training colleges in Kenya were preparing 5,700 teacher students for grade schools, and 400 for high schools. But there is still a shortage of teachers in secondary schools, especially in natural science subjects. The Kenya's Teachers' Service Commission is the one employer for over 30,000 teachers—or *Mwalimu*, the Swahili word for "Schoolteacher." The Commission sends out appeals to college students who are working towards degrees in Europe and America, to consider filling the breach. It pays a salary, plus tuition and a book allowance, to graduate students who undertake the one-year teacher-training course when they return home.

For some years before Kenya gained independence, sponsors brought promising students to American colleges and universities. One private program drew worldwide attention when it organized "student airlift," and started bringing groups of students by chartered planes to American colleges and universities that had offered them scholarships. During December, 1959, the first plane to leave Nairobi with eighty-one students was farewelled by thousands of cheering well-wishers. But the second consignment of 136 students drew even bigger exuberant crowds to the Nairobi airport, for it was the first time a jet plane was used on such a project.

In 1960, the African Scholarship Program of American Universities (ASPAU) began with offers of scholarships from twenty-four American colleges and universities—a number which quickly rose to 250. The institutions provide free tuition for four years, and the United States Government finances room, board, books, and recreation. By the end of 1962, students from Kenya numbering 1,592 had benefited from the plan which is still in operation.

One non-profit organization that is deeply concerned in helping African nations solve their educational, economic, and social problems is the African-American Institute. AAI is directed by a Board of Trustees of American philanthropists who are active in civil rights and higher education. It was founded in 1954. Since that year AAI has tripled its staff and revised its program several times to meet Africa's changing needs.

By 1966, Kenyans numbered 943 of 2,000 African students that AAI had placed in American colleges and uni-

Miss Wangari Muta (seated), sent by AAI to study in American veterinary colleges, is an assistant lecturer at Nairobi's University College.

versities. Of this number, 123 were sponsored by the United States Government, 117 by private persons, 105 by the students themselves, and the remainder by the Kenyan Government, or the colleges they attended, or a combination of both.

AAI maintains an office in East Africa that works closely with a government committee in Nairobi that controls scholarship funds and interviews prospective candidates for study abroad. The committee's choice is influenced by an applicant's previous academic achievement and his foreseeable ability, upon graduation, to fill high-level posts in deficient areas of Kenya. If the prospective student receives a scholarship he is bonded to serve in a specified field within Kenya's Public Service. Should a student need additional financial aid while in America, in an emergency the Kenya Government gives him short-term assistance or a full scholarship until completion of his studies. It also gives assistance for medical expenses.

A survey of subject preferences made in 1966 shows that Kenyan students favor Social Science subjects, though the Humanities and Physical and Natural Sciences follow as a close second. When students have outstanding academic abilities in their chosen subject and can receive financial outside support, the Kenyan Government encourages them, upon graduation, to continue their studies in America. But the Government withdraws its support if a student defaults or unadvisably changes his course of study. And rather than have students return to Kenya as vacationists during the summer months (which is time that can better be used for study or earning money in temporary work), the Govern-

A class in husbandry with a cow that has just calved at a demonstration farm.

ment publishes a monthly newsletter in America that keeps a recipient up to date on events at home which include the job opportunities that await him when he returns.

The Kenya Government must be sure that the privileged students who are sent abroad acquire skills that are necessary to the country's progress. His Excellency Mr. Burudi Nabwera, Kenya's Ambassador in Washington, stressed the diversity in social philosophy that exists between his country and America. At a conference in Washington he said,

". . . In the United States, emphasis is placed on the rights of the individual. In Africa, the community has priority. We believe that the individual should consider the welfare of the community as a whole before stressing what he considers to be his individual privileges . . ."

AAI cooperates in placing young men and women in the right colleges where their particular talents find full scope for expression, and it supplies a Training and Development Program that gives students working experience to help them when they return home. As one of several private agencies that strengthens relationship and understanding between Kenya and America, AAI performs a major service.

Education for young Kenyans in academic and technical subjects is rightly recognized as an urgency in the Harambee nation-building program, and more than 4,000 students are placed in the colleges and universities of almost twenty foreign countries with the Government's sanction. But the Government has not yet given its support to Kenya's culture. Music, drama, literature, and the visual arts are in the hands of a few competent, dedicated people who strive to preserve the various art forms that are already highly developed.

There are art schools and music schools, theaters and cultural centers in Kenya, but the main interest is focused on the non-profit art gallery and studio in Nairobi called *Paa-Ya-Paa*—a Swahili word meaning "The Antelope Rises." As Mr. Elimo, the gallery's director, says, ". . . We hope the antelope rises into a new realm of . . . creative adventures that will give full scope for the free expression of the artist."

Art students exhibit their work at the gallery if it is acceptable, and students of literature exhibit their writings during the Annual Book Week Fair. A competent group of playwrights produce their plays, performed by Theater Paa-Ya-Paa, and camera addicts show their photographs, including documentary films.

Kenya's painters work in bold, strong color, mainly in a semi-abstract style, though sometimes the paintings portray their traditional backgrounds. Sculptors work just as powerfully whether they carve in wood or mold in clay.

Craft centers are scattered throughout the country, one of the most productive being located near Machakos. Wakamba wood carvings are exported and sold in countries around the world. "Airport Art," as the center's products are commonly called, are a big tourist attraction as well as being a lucrative industry that earns the Government a large foreign exchange revenue. But the serious Kenya artists deplore the millions of little carvings of giraffes, antelope, salad bowls, and servers that find their way into foreign homes. To them it is Kenya art that has been misapplied and exploited.

While some Kenyan students yearn to absorb Western academic and technical skills, art students yearn to enrich the world with Kenyan art in its original, unspoiled form.

10

HARAMBEE
AND HEALTH

Kenya's Development Plan under African Socialism has
fired the people with a desire to cooperate in improving still
further the splendid health services the Government supplies. There is now a national awareness of the importance
of better health habits and nutrition since the people in
both rural areas and larger communities entered into a self-
help program. The combined building efforts of the volunteers resulted in new health centers and dispensaries.
The people also solicit money for their maintenance and for
new hospital wards and maternity wings. Kenyans do not
hesitate to patronize the new services, nor do nomadic tribespeople spurn the mobile clinics that tour their provinces.
Outpatients who attend government hospitals and all children who enter them receive free medical care.

Despite the tremendous efforts the Government makes in

bringing modern medicine to the people, and an increase of
$1½ million in the Ministry of Health budget in 1967,
Kenya must turn to outside help in providing many needed
services because of lack of funds. Mission hospitals and
other private enterprises are active in Kenya, but even they
face difficulties in keeping within their budgets with a
quickly expanding population. That the country is dependent to a high degree on gifts and grants is considered a
temporary necessity during the transition period in Kenya's
Development Plan.

July, 1967, saw the commencement of a Medical School
in Nairobi under the auspices of the University College of
East Africa. By training one hundred students locally each
year there will be a considerable saving in funds. The World
Health Organization (WHO) is interested in the project
and recommended that $1 million was necessary for basic
minimum facilities, and about $800,000 per year for main-
tenance allowing $3,000 annually for each student. The
Glasgow University (Scotland) assisted in the project
through Britain's Ministry of Overseas Development.

The Ministry of Health concentrates on preventive medicine. For instance, Kenya's record of polio outbreaks follows
a triennial pattern. The British Government donated 3 million vaccine shots which were used all over the country to
forestall the next epidemic, which is due in 1969. There
have been other successful campaigns, supported by WHO
and the United Nations International Children's Emergency
Fund (UNICEF), to defeat disease at its source before it
gains a deadly grip.

Of the government hospitals in Kenya, the Kenyatta National Hospital in Nairobi compares with Africa's best in size and modern equipment. In mid-July, 1964, government hospitals had a total of 6,931 beds, mission hospitals had 3,091, and private hospitals had 1,589. These numbers have greatly increased in the years since independence. A new obstetric wing and extensions to the hospital's nursing home are being built, and the British Government is financing a training school which will provide Kenya with nurses who are important to the overall successful conclusion to Kenya's better health campaign.

Listed among a nurse's duties are periodic visits to rural districts with working teams from the Ministry of Health. They administer medical care and teach the people how to protect themselves from infectious diseases. Visiting teams from the Agriculture Department advise on how to grow nutritious foods. Malnutrition, one serious problem that afflicts Kenya's people, results mainly from ignorance and

The Kenyatta National Hospital in Nairobi.

antiquated farming methods that do not produce the right foods. The children, especially, need better care—nourishing foods that will strengthen them, build their resistance to sickness, and prepare them for the advanced education and, later, the remunerative jobs that Harambee has made available. The Government has undertaken the big task of correcting the lamentable condition through application and education.

The Ministry of Health interested one private company in producing a protein supplementary food, now distributed to rural schools that have a lunch program. The mixture contains dried milk, yeast, and barley flour, and is fortified with vitamin A and iodine. Parents of children who attend schools

Women of a coastal tribe churn milk near a rural collection point.

that provide the food have been made conscious of the need for body-building foods. They have been led to reformed habits, not by scoldings, but by demonstration. In many instances parents have started growing beans and peas and other green vegetables to add to their children's diets.

Nairobi's City Council and the Kenya Cooperative Creameries give fresh milk free to 6,500 children every day, and the Government has asked rural dairies to supply their neighborhood schools and nurseries with fresh skimmed milk. And to fill a need, UNICEF built two milk plants that produce dried skimmed milk which the personnel allots to pregnant women and nursing mothers.

A modern butter churn provided by UNICEF at the Mariakani milk plant near Mombasa.

The Kenya Government recognizes the country's potentialities for food production and regards what help it receives from foreign sources as temporary. Under Harambee, Kenya looks forward to when it will be free of the necessity to depend on outside help for the right foods and their distribution.

Because of its limited resources, Kenya's Government depends on voluntary agencies in the fields of welfare and social services. This presents no problem for by tradition mutual help is rooted deeply in Kenya's people. The system, always strong within families and the tribes, now includes the nation. It is Uhuru na Umoja in action.

Some fifty voluntary organizations coordinate their efforts through the Kenya National Council of Social Service which is the link with the Government though not the recipient of government financial aid. Formerly, agencies such as the Red Cross and the Salvation Army were branches of international organizations and received funds from overseas; now they, like other member agencies, are supported by private donation within the nation.

Social workers are alert to emergencies. They hurry to homes when they learn of sudden illness. They tend the children of a sick mother, and comfort those who are bereaved or perhaps deserted and destitute. Voluntary social and welfare workers advise the National Health Insurance Scheme in extreme instances which then relieves the burden of medical expenses. Upon their recommendation, a National Provident Fund feeds the poor. The good works of the kind people who give their services cannot be too loudly acclaimed. They are friends who never fail the needy.

Like any new nation that is undergoing complete upheaval
in its governing policies, sometimes Kenya suffers from disruption in its precious family life. It is understandable that
big towns and cities act as lures to rural dwellers when they
hear of their busy, feverish progress. It happens everywhere
that young people, especially boys, are apt to desert their
homes for the excitement of modern city life. In Kenya
boys gravitate towards Nairobi. Gangs of hungry, homeless
boys roamed the streets until recently. They begged for
food and slept in alleyways. Their problems were solved
when the Kenya National Youth Service established the
Starehe Boys Center. *Starehe* means "Welfare" in the Swahili language. Credit goes to the welfare workers who started
the venture when they rescued boys from the streets, perhaps from lives of crime, and gave them shelter in one small
shed. Today, Starehe is a $75,000-a-year concern located
in the middle of Nairobi's poor district. By private donation
(and donations from bigger organizations such as the Ford
Foundation, Nuffield Foundation, and the Save the Children
Fund) it maintains grade, high, and technical schools, and
accommodates three hundred permanent boarders and two
hundred day students. Homeless, hungry boys no longer
roam Nairobi's streets.

Kenya's medical services assure good health; its social and
welfare workers ease the strain of living. Both improved
conditions are conducive to progress. So, too, is the physical
recreation program that is included in the new nation's program. Sports play a large part in the Harambee scheme, and
the Government supports the National Council of Sport of
which President Kenyatta is chief patron.

When Kenyans lived as tribes they had no organized sport, though they wrestled, practiced spear-throwing and bow-shooting, ran great distances, and climbed mountains. Europeans introduced games and sports. Kenyans learned quickly, not only on the home ground, but in international competition also. In swimming, field hockey, boxing, and Rugby football (which is virtually the national sport) they excel, but in running Kenyans outdistance the rest of the world.

Kipchoge Keino, a 26-year-old policeman, holds two world records in track races. In 1965, Keino won the World Games Silver Medal at Haelsmborg in Finland when he smashed the 3,000-metres record by covering the distance in 7 minutes, 39.5 seconds. A few days later he covered the one-mile race in England in 3 minutes, 54.2 seconds.

Kipchoge Keino, holder of two world records in track.

It seems that Kipchoge Keino was merely warming to the challenge. In 1966, he toured New Zealand and there established a new world record for the 5,000-metre race with a time of 13 minutes, 24.2 seconds. And of eight races in New Zealand he won six and finished second in the other two. He went on to further victories in Australia where he set a new record of 8 minutes, 25.2 seconds in one two-mile race.

Keino visited America where he twice won the two-mile indoor race—first in Los Angeles, later at Madison Square Garden in New York. One sportswriter describes him as being the "greatest runner Africa has ever produced."

Kipchoge Keino is the standard-bearer for Kenya. But there are other Kenyans in the world of sport who are ready in their special fields to follow the path he has blazed as a champion runner.

Self-help in communities is fitted into the Development Plan. It is seen as an integral and necessary part of Kenya's scheme for growth and is carefully controlled to conserve the energies of volunteers, and to channel them into constructive projects to benefit as many people as possible. Some groups help to improve old roads and nudge new ones into remote areas and thus make them more accessible. Other groups concentrate their efforts in building better homes and raising the living standards of the people. Tremendous strides have been made in clearing undesirable slum areas near the cities, and replacing old shacks with new, clean homes. Where overcrowding impeded progress, families were persuaded to move (over the new roads) and relocate in areas that have been opened when their resources were increased.

Preventive medicines, nourishing foods, healthy sports, and better housing have succeeded in lowering Kenya's mortality rate so that population numbers are leaping in excess of 3 percent yearly. Already more than half of Kenya's people are under sixteen years of age. President Kenyatta looks far into the future. At the present rate of population increase, he reckons, 7 million jobs will be needed by the year 2000 for the 230,000 adult males who will, by that time, be added to the labor force each year. There will be 6 million school children to care for and many more dependents than the country can comfortably support. Future Development Plans will be hampered and adequate social and welfare services will be difficult. Progress will stop unless something is done to control the growing population.

So Mr. Kenyatta includes family planning in the Harambee program. Knowledgeable councillors from the Family Planning Association enlighten receptive parents on the wisdom of having smaller families. "The number of children you want when you want them," is the Association's slogan. Councillors stress the happiness that comes with healthy, adequately fed and clothed children, a condition possible when there are no more children as part of a family than the father can support.

The supervisors of Kenya's health program are aware of the emergencies that could interfere with their Development Plan. By proceeding cautiously, they are confident that the year 2000 will see a healthy people of a number that will no more than balance Kenya's increased food production.

11

THE BIGGEST ZOO

East Africa has the largest concentration of wild animals in the world, and Kenya's eight national parks attract well over 150,000 visitors every year. The visitors who view the vast herds of unhurried, seemingly tame animals have made tourism Kenya's second largest source of revenue. They not only spend money, but they also ease Kenya's unemployment, making wildlife every bit as vital as agriculture to Kenya's economy. President Kenyatta expects that the annual income from visitors will exceed $75 million by 1970, and that more than 60,000 trained personnel will be needed to serve them. Tourists have already booked space through Kenya's new Tourist Development Corporation three or four years in advance and the Government, in preparation for the influx, has built new lodges and numerous roads that follow the trails of grazing and browsing animals.

Each lodge in a reserve has a view, either of mountains, the Rift Valley, or a lake that vibrates with colorful birds.

Every moment of a visitor's stay is packed with excitement of an unexpected and thrilling nature, and often right at hand. Visitors scanning the view from a lodge balcony are quite apt to glimpse a lioness relaxing with her fluffy, yellow cubs—a scene that physically resembles the layout of a lodge, which is a group of buildings consisting of a large lounge and dining room with separate, individual guest cottages clustered around the central unit.

The Nairobi National Park is Kenya's smallest park. It lies within five miles of the city and covers a little more than forty square miles. Until access to the park was made easier with good roads, many city children had never seen their country's precious heritage of animals. Now, minibuses convey them to the Nairobi Animal Orphanage, which is

A young leopard at the Nairobi Animal Orphanage.

right at the park's entrance, for briefing before they enter the park. With the aid of movies and colored slides, the children receive a thorough coaching in how to recognize the different species of fauna. To arouse their interest still further, they are taught the habits of animals and how one species is dependent upon another for survival and that *all* animals are important to people and should be protected.

The Orphanage was started by Mr. C. E. Cade when a newborn bushbuck was brought to him after being rescued by a sympathetic warden from the clutches of a baboon. In 1963, the Orphanage was officially opened with thirty-two baby animals that had been either orphaned, separated from their mothers, or abandoned. It now houses 120 animals consisting of over forty species. When the young animal charges reach adult age they are not merely turned loose to fend for themselves. Orphanage curators train them to take their places alongside their own kind in the wilds. Sometimes an animal refuses to leave the Orphanage; then it is sold to a zoo.

There are three reasons for providing such a sanctuary where the young of antelopes, cheetahs, wild dogs, leopards, wildebeeste, buffalo, and lions frolic together. It saves their lives, it is a unique means of educating Kenya's people to conserve wildlife, and its research station is a valuable addition for study by students from East African universities in ecology and its related subjects.

When visitors choose early morning to drive into the park they see the world changing from gray to silver. As the waxing light touches the wide savannahs it discloses literally thousands of unconcerned animals placidly going about the business of eating breakfast. Patchwork giraffes, so huge and gentle, pose in picturesque groups as they nibble new leaves from spreading acacias. Perhaps Nairobi's modern skyline forms the background, brought deceptively close by the clean morning air.

Candy-striped zebra graze in single file. They and countless numbers of Kenya's forty species of antelope, move and live in peace as if the Flood were just over and they had come only that morning out of Noah's Ark. That a pride of lions (sometimes thirty in number) relaxes in their midst heightens the atmosphere of mutual trust. The lions and the cheetahs have finished their nocturnal feasting and the leopards have carried their prey out of reach in the trees, but the scavengers—hyenas, jackals, vultures, and marabou storks—are busily gnawing and pecking at whatever has been left for them. When the scavengers are satiated and move away the ants take over and pick the bones

Giraffe beside a lake in the Rift Valley.

Zebra on the run.

A rare black-maned lion.

white. Thus, nature's plan keeps the savannahs free of the refuse that brings disease.

Kenya's resident and migrant bird count reaches 1,500 different species. Overhead, varieties of eagles soar effortlessly, and vultures rise and dip like so many pieces of black paper tossed by a breeze. With luck a visitor might see a Hartlands' bustard fly straight up and then drop, heavily, like a stone.

When tourists drive through one of the few forests in the park they move under a great canopy of trees. Wisps of mist coil through vines and creepers, dew dampens the air. The forest is silent except for the piping of many birds and the shrill squeaks of young colobus monkeys. There is a feeling of being watched, but except for the whisk of a vanishing tail or the flash of a retreating rump, one does not see animals. In the wooded areas they move from sight with scarcely the stir of a leaf. When passing a stream through the forest a honking Hammerhead stork (*Scopus umbretta*) may look down from his huge domed nest fashioned from sticks made fast with mud. This species of stork builds the largest nest in Africa, sufficiently sturdy to support a man.

In tropical East Africa the black night closes in quickly, like a falling curtain. The visitors have left the park before dark for the night belongs to predators.

Each of Kenya's national parks has its own individual characteristics. In contrast to the smallness and intimacy of the Nairobi National Park, Tsavo is large and sprawling. It covers over 8,000 square miles of rugged, wild country that straddles the main road and railroad between Nairobi and Mombasa. Within Tsavo National Park roam the big-

A charging bull elephant.

A herd of buffalo.

Young black rhinoceroses.

gest of the wild game—lions, buffalo, and rhinoceroses. Elephants, which are absent in Nairobi's park, are numerous in Tsavo. At Mzima Springs in Tsavo, visitors watch from a vast underwater glass tank, twenty feet long, the antics of hippopotamuses and crocodiles, and a darting myriad of colorful fish.

Tsavo National Park is adjacent to the Kenya coast. It is to Kilindini that rhinoceros horns from hundreds of animals slaughtered by poachers are smuggled, and from that port they are shipped to countries of the Far East. The peoples of China and Southeast Asia make love potions from rhino horn which they erroneously believe has an aphrodisiac quality. Today, a rhino horn fetches $28 a pound in a disastrously active traffic which is handled mainly by Arabs.

No one knows for how many centuries the trade in rhino

horns has existed, or how long the outside world has had knowledge of East Africa's unique wildlife, but it is recorded that when Emperor Yung Lo (of the Ming dynasty in China) heard of giraffes, he sent a ship to the port of Malindi early in the fifteenth century to fetch one. The giraffe's description resembled that of one Chinese legendary beast, the *k'-lin*, having "the body of a deer, the tail of a cow, ate only vegetable matter, and was gentle in demeanor." The captain of the Emperor's ship acquired the giraffe and a zebra, the first of their species to delight the Chinese people. Today, of course, every foreign zoo features examples of both animals.

In 1909, when big-game hunting was fast becoming a popular international sport, President Theodore Roosevelt went on a two-week foot safari that started from Nairobi. It was a splendid procession. Following a flag-bearer were the President, 265 porters, horses, and wagons carrying supplies and sixty-four tents.

Although President Roosevelt was an ardent hunter, his voice was one of several that succeeded in founding the New York Zoological Society in 1895. The new Society's prime interest was to preserve the world's wildlife. One clause in the original charter states that the Society "was to be a force for the conservation of wildlife . . . so man can conserve life within nature."

The Society has strived through the years to live by the charter's principles, yet for every one of the seemingly endless streams of wild animals in Kenya today, there were fifty at the turn of the century. The part played by big-game hunters in depleting their numbers is negligible compared to the demands by farmers for more land, or the practices of poachers.

In April, 1924, Sir Robert Corydon, who was at that time Kenya's governor, protested the smuggling of rhino horns and elephant tusks through the free ports of Barawa and Mogadiscio in Somalia (then Italian Somaliland) to the value of $200,000 annually. The nefarious traffic also found an outlet equally large through Zanzibar off the Tanzania coast. So eager were poachers for the spoils of smuggling that they drove back pursuing game wardens with arrows tipped with poison from a local tree, *Acokanthera friesiorum*.

The rich rewards gained by poaching saw an increase in the practice. By 1930, the number of wild animals in Kenya were reduced to ten for every one today. Leopards were persecuted for their handsome skins and one investigation disclosed $15,000 as the price for a Somali leopard-skin coat on a furrier's rack. Leopards are valuable in keeping down such pests as crop-destroying baboons. To keep nature's balance the law protects them. Big-game hunters must have a license to shoot leopards, and there is a low limit on the number they can take.

Many Mau Mau leaders, trained to be game wardens, proved themselves relentless pursuers of poachers. During an antipoaching drive of 1956-1957 wardens succeeded in finding 117 hideouts and 1,292 trapped and killed elephants over a ten-week period. At the same time the wardens recovered 444 tusks weighing 8,500 pounds of ivory.

Poachers benefited when man's means of hunting game became more scientific. In 1960, tranquilizing darts were in-

A National Park Ranger.

troduced, primarily as a way of conveying animals to less crowded areas or for studying their body functioning more closely (such as listening to an elephant's heartbeat) which is only possible while a wild animal is unconscious. The drugs used to incapacitate animals need skillful handling and must be followed by neutralizing drugs, otherwise animals die under the tranquilizer. Or if an animal is not followed into the wilds when in a doped state and protected, it can become the prey of predators.

When ecologists made a careful count of Tsavo Park's rhino population and found that it was less than the park could support, they brought in several animals from a crowded area. First the ecologists shot a dart into the rhino; then they carried it by helicopter to its new home, where they administered the antidote and awakened the animal to music. Each operation of transporting a rhino costs approximately $1,000. But traders who illegally capture wild animals for sale to zoos use tranquilizing darts indiscriminately, and it is estimated that only one animal in eight survives the ordeal.

The majority of Kenya's seventy-five licensed hunters have replaced *shooting* safaris with *camera* safaris. While conducting their clients through big game areas they also assist the police in capturing suspected poachers. The penalties are much harsher since Uhuru, and fines for poaching can be as high as $2,800 or five years in prison.

Poaching practices decimate Kenya's animal population, but an even bigger menace is the very presence of man, and man's cattle. When there were fewer people and more wild animals in Kenya, an ancient harmony existed between

A Kenya Police Air Wing plane directing Game Rangers toward poachers sighted from the air.

man and beast. They and the vegetation complemented each other. But the coming of outsiders into Kenya upset the balance. Arabs introduced the greed for wealth gained by illicit trade; Europeans introduced modern medicine which shot Kenya's population figure beyond what the land could support. Wild-game numbers dwindled as herders overgrazed the savannahs, cleared the forests, and followed shifting cultivation and scorched earth policies. The hooves of domestic cattle destroyed the soil's porous structure, turning it to dust and thus exposing it to erosion by rain and wind. Cattle monopolized the watering places, resulting in the deaths of thousands of wild animals from thirst. When elephants trampled the cornfields, lions and leopards raided farmyards, and buffalo crashed fences, a sort of undeclared war started between the people and their valuable irreplaceable animals. To Kenyans, wild animals were *nyama* only, which means "meat." It was uphill work indeed for Kenya's Ministry of Tourism and Wildlife when it started educating the people under the new Development Plan. As an instance of the difficulties, one shop window display in the education campaign showed a leopard caught in a cruel trap. Beside it were guns and other diabolical forms of destruction, and a fine leopard-skin coat. But until they understood the message the display conveyed, the throng of people who crowded around the window were only interested in where they could buy such a powerful trap.

But Kenyans learn quickly. Through tutoring by the African Wildlife Leadership Foundation they are now cognizant of the importance of saving the animals that have been so generously bestowed on their country. AWLF contributes $500,000 annually in establishing and maintaining centers where conservationists teach methods of preserving Kenya's number one asset, and conserving for the pleasure of future generations what can never be replaced if it is annihilated.

Kenya's farmers need one-quarter of the land at present, but with the increase in population in thirty years they will need one-half of the land. To make this possible without destroying the wildlife requires careful, complex planning. Worldwide organizations and individuals aid Kenya's conservation scheme in maintaining the reserves and in opening new ones where the distribution and balance of animals can be closely observed and regulated. The New York Zoological Society and its affiliate, the Conservation Foundation, are active participants. The Foundation sends expert conservation advisors to Kenya. Aware that green grass and water are the secrets of abundance, the Foundation sinks wells in Tsavo Park, some of which are 300 feet deep. Small diesel engines drive pumps that bring water to storage tanks and automatic gravity feeds that lead to concrete drinking pools. It also builds bridges as easier access to wildlife by game wardens, and it provides patrol aircraft.

One aerial count over Tsavo Park showed 20,000 elephants confined to an area that could not support so large a number, though it was normally one that possessed good forage. The elephants had suffered the squeeze of man's need for land and were starving. Moreover, their density threatened the survival of other fauna within the park, especially the black rhino which share the same habitat.

With the consent of Kenya's Ministry of Tourism and

A water hole in the Tsavo National Park.

Wildlife, the Ford Foundation provided a grant of $200,000 for a three-year research program which included a study of every aspect of elephant biology, and the effects of both fire and elephant on the vegetation. After a research unit had carefully studied the situation, it recommended shooting 300 elephants. In the interests of conservation it is necessary, sometimes, to destroy.

When *Born Free*, the book by Joy Adamson, burst upon the world in twenty-one languages and was read by 100 million responsive readers, it probably stimulated more interest in wildlife conservation than any other known form of publicity. In the book the author tells the story of Elsa, the lion cub she took into her home, and to her heart, in unemotional but warm detail. She raised the cub and with the help of her husband trained Elsa to live as a lion rather than as a domestic pet before returning her to face wildlife alone.

Mrs. Adamson is the wife of George Adamson, Kenya's Senior Game Warden of the arid Northern Frontier District. Together they go on safaris. While her husband attends to his duties, Mrs. Adamson collects ethnographic, botanic, entomologic, and anthropologic material for Nairobi's Corydon Museum. Her watercolor paintings of indigenous peoples, flora, and fauna, are graphic records of a Kenya that is gradually changing. Though Joy Adamson was born in Austria she is a fine example of a loyal and patriotic Kenyan citizen, making valuable contributions to the growth of a new nation.

Almost as remarkable as knowing a lion intimately was the making of the film of Elsa's story, also called *Born Free*. A husband and wife team undertook to play the precarious leading roles. They needed great funds of patience in establishing a rapport with their co-star, and courage when their pride of lions behaved at times like lions rather than movie stars. The Kenya Government cooperated in making possible the beautiful color photography and in making available the more docile of their animals. When *Born Free* had its American premiere in Washington, D.C., the proceeds were donated to the World Wildlife Fund.

There are always stories circulated that pertain to special occasions, and Elsa was not spared. One was told of a scene in a theater in Nairobi. The characters were a woman, an American tourist who sat behind her, and the woman's pet lion. They were watching *Born Free*. The lion sat straight and still, staring at the screen. The tourist, in dumbfounded awe, stared at the lion's engrossment. At last, the tourist could no longer contain his curiosity and tapped the woman

Filming Born Free *in Kenya.*

on the shoulder. "Is she enjoying it?" he asked, and the woman replied, "I don't know, but she liked the book."

Now that the world is aware of the urgency to preserve the last accessible remnant of wildlife that has survived a million years of evolution, visitors enter Kenya's parks with a strong feeling of empathy. And the animals seem to respond. They are less startled and suspicious, they are more relaxed and calm. They *seem* to turn and smile a welcome. Perhaps, in the words of Joy Adamson, "The great barrier between man and the world of wild animals can be breached by patience, affection, and a little imagination."

The world's biggest zoo in its noble setting will continue to bring joy to visitors for a further million years of evolution if the people observe the rules of preservation.

12

EAST AFRICAN COOPERATION

President Kenyatta looked to the future when he studied means of strengthening the wide scope of East African territory through unity. He decided that the spirit of Harambee could be extended to included Tanzania and Uganda, two countries that had traveled a similar course to Kenya's—from being British Protectorates to fully independent nations.

Prior to their independence Kenya, Tanzania, and Uganda were run under the East African High Commission. As the three participating countries achieved Uhuru, in its turn the common market as it then existed became invalid except in a few instances. It was replaced by the East African Common Services Organization (E.A.C.S.O.) which provided some twenty common services for the three countries, ranging from their railroads, harbors, and post offices, to medical and veterinary services. It also included the collecting of revenue from income taxes, customs, and excise duties. President Kenyatta was ambitious to expand the common services still farther.

In August, 1966, the three East African Governments set up a Commission to examine the possibilities of forming a new East African Common Market, and how such a market could be controlled and regulated. Three Ministers from each of the three states comprised the Commission which was under the Chairmanship of Professor K. Philip of Denmark, who came from the United Nations in New York. The Commission studied several points, such as the distribution of headquarters for existing services and the establishing of new services and arranging for their financial, legal, and administrative handling before it submitted a report in May, 1967. A treaty was drafted from the report, and early in June the three heads of state—President Jomo Kenyatta of Kenya, President Julius Nyerere of Tanzania, and Dr. Milton Obote of Uganda—met in Kampala, Uganda. There they signed the Treaty of East African Cooperation, the terms of which were put into effect early in December, 1967.

The new East African Community, comprised of the three integrated Governments, is similar to the European Economic Community in Brussels. All three countries share a common tariff against the outside world. The common market side of the treaty maintains common customs and excise taxes, external trade policies, and freedom of transit between the three countries. The common services side of the treaty includes four corporations that run the railroads, harbors, mails and telegraph, and airways between all three countries. Twelve basic research institutes deal with fundamental problems in medicine, natural resources, and industrial development.

A Secretariat with its headquarters at Arusha in Tanzania directs the new Community. The Harbor Department is located in Dar-es-Salaam in Tanzania; Post and Telegraph services and a new East African Development bank are in Kampala; while Airways, Railroads, and the Court of Appeals remain in Kenya.

When Mr. Kenyatta had signed the treaty he returned to Nairobi and spoke with pleasure and confidence to the mass of his people. "Our East African Community . . . is indeed one of the most advanced states of cooperation between Sovereign states anywhere in the world," he said. "We have something of which we can be proud."

The East African Community offers a market of nearly 30 million people to overseas investors, a circumstance that is becoming more and more the focus of attention from foreign business. Its easy functioning also interests neighboring countries such as Ethiopia and Zambia, whose Governments see the advantages of such a Community. That they, too, will become participants in the Development Plan under Harambee is now under consideration.

Harambee—"Let's all pull together"—reached Kenya's young people. It inspired them to organize "Harambee Africa," which brought 950 students from fourteen African countries to a conference in Nairobi. They decided to form musical groups as a practical means of conveying through song and dance the unity that comes by hard work.

Self-help groups also gave practical demonstrations at the meeting in Nairobi. President Kenyatta, pleased when he witnessed one group as it helped in the construction of a stretch of roadway, commented that ". . . You set a good example because in many countries young educated men grow up without wanting to dirty their hands; they don't like getting the dirt behind their fingernails. When you go back to your homes, villages, and countries, do this every day, not just once a year, but every day. If you do this it will help us build a new Africa." So the young people, encouraged by the President's message, set up self-help projects in their own countries or Kenyan villages when they returned to their homes.

The members of "Harambee Africa" in Kenya are mainly high-school and teacher training college students. The competent troupe of performers traveled all over East Africa, presenting a program before the youth of other lands, and leaving behind them so much enthusiasm that "Harambee Moshi" was organized in Tanzania, and "Voice of Tomorrow" in Uganda. As their fame spread, the performers were invited by the Governments of Sudan and Ethiopia to bring the spirit of Harambee to their countries also.

"Harambee Africa" is one of more than thirty youth organizations in Kenya that operate under the guidance of a Youth Council. In October, 1966, they combined in a week-long Youth Festival in Nairobi. Over 8,000 representative young African citizens took part in activities that included exciting dances and sports events, massed bands that led parades, fashion shows in the new Independence Hall along with displays of art, industries, and the professions. The purpose of the festival was truly in the spirit of Harambee, for the organizers distributed all the gate receipts to Nairobi's

A Luo girl in the Kenya national dress.

impoverished children through the school luncheon scheme.

Kenya's young people are fully aware of the magical results attained in nation-building under Harambee. They see that cooperation brings success in every branch of government—in the preservation of their country's wildlife, in improved farming, in housing and health services on the home front and the diligence of Kenya's representatives in their country's foreign services.

It is not surprising that a "new" African personality is emerging, that Kenyans reaching adulthood are free of the oppressions and doubts under which their parents labored while conforming to alien standards. Young Kenyans step into the future proud and confident in the knowledge that they can contribute to the general human culture in a purely African sense.

At the closing of the Youth Festival, President Kenyatta spoke aptly when he told his large audience of eager young people, "Youth with a purpose is a theme with a stirring challenge. . . . The future is bright with promise and it is in your determination that the greatness and prosperity of Kenya lies."

The beautiful land of Kenya will continue to grow and to flourish under such inspired guidance and so united and enthusiastic a people. Kenya will be the shining example that leads a new Africa along the road to full achievement.

INDEX